Should I stay or should I go?

JIM BRIGHT

Should I stay or should I go?

How to make that crucial
job move decision

London • New York • Toronto • Sydney • Tokyo • Singapore
Hong Kong • Cape Town • Madrid • Paris • Amsterdam • Munich • Milan

PEARSON EDUCATION LIMITED

Head Office:
Edinburgh Gate
Harlow CM20 2JE
Tel: +44 (0)1279 623623
Fax: +44 (0)1279 431059

London Office:
128 Long Acre
London WC2E 9AN
Tel: +44 (0)20 7447 2000
Fax: +44 (0)20 7447 2170
Website: www.business-minds.com
        www.yourmomentum.com

First published in Great Britain in 2003

© Pearson Education Limited 2003

The right of Jim Bright to be identified as Author of this Work has been asserted by him in accordance with the Copyright, Designs and Patents Act 1988.

ISBN 0 273 66301 1

British Library Cataloguing in Publication Data
A CIP catalogue record for this book can be obtained from the British Library

10 9 8 7 6 5 4 3

Typeset by Northern Phototypesetting Co. Ltd, Bolton
Printed and bound in Great Britain by Bell & Bain Ltd, Glasgow

The Publishers' policy is to use paper manufactured from sustainable forests.

Dedication

For Benjamin Mark John Bright.

'When choosing between two evils, I always pick the one I haven't tried before.'
Mae West

Contents

Acknowledgements

There are so many people who have helped put this book together or have developed my thinking in this area. Thanks to Vera Thomson for typing up my in-car dictated notes. Thanks to the School of Psychology, UNSW, for providing me with opportunity to write this book, to the School of Psychology, Macquarie University, for playing host to me during most of the writing process. I am particularly indebted to friends and colleagues who have provided ideas and stimulated my thinking in this area. They include: Robert Pryor, Jo Earl, Lene Jensen, Sharon Wilkenfeld, Sue Pedri and Robert Bright. Finally, thanks to my wife and business partner, Karen, and my sons, William and Ben, for putting up with my working long and sometimes strange hours!

Jim Bright, Bayview, December 2002

Introduction

This book aims to assist you with the most critical of all career questions that many, if not all of us, have asked at least once in our lives: *Should I stay in my job or should I leave?*

Maybe you are sitting there with another job offer on the table and are trying to weigh it up. Maybe you are just mildly dissatisfied with your job and thinking about whether it's time to cast about and look for something new. Maybe you are wondering if you've been in the job too long and ought to move to avoid stagnation. Maybe you want more money. Maybe somebody has told you that you should get out because the company is on the rocks. Maybe you've hit a ceiling and although you don't want to move, you know you might have to in order to get on. Maybe you can't stand your boss and wonder if it's enough reason to move on. Maybe you think you want to go and do something completely different but don't know what or how or, indeed, if you should.

There are myriad reasons why you could be asking yourself 'should I stay or should I go?' but whatever the reason, this book can help. It will help you work out where you are in your career, what's good and what's bad about your current job and whether that means you should stay – or go.

It's a good first sign that you have picked up this book. It's increasingly important and relevant for more of us to be asking questions about our careers, because we are all having to take more responsibility for our own career management. The days of the paternal employer who looked after all your employment needs from the cradle to the grave are pretty much in the past. Some industries such as IT have pioneered self-management of career issues. In other industries such as banking and finance where there once existed stable employment and clearly delineated career paths, we now see tremendous global upheaval and a focus on management for shareholders rather than for employees. This has resulted in job insecurity, a breakdown of mutual trust between employee and employer and a recognition by both parties that the only person who will look out for your career is you.

The underlying philosophy of this book is that you are ultimately responsible for your own career management and destiny. This means that you should:

- take responsibility for your career decisions
- look for opportunities to develop
- develop a reasonable understanding of where on the world career map you want to head for or, at the very least, where you want to avoid
- recognize that events can overtake the best plans and be prepared to capitalize on chance
- recognize what is within your control (and worth working on) and what is outside your control (and therefore not worth worrying about).

Throughout this book there are many quizzes and audits. These quizzes are designed to help you reflect on your decision-making. The interpretation of these quizzes should serve to provide the stimulus for your own thinking.

Good luck!

Jim Bright

'We are so happy to advise others that occasionally we even do it in their interest.'

Jules Renard, author

PART ONE

Getting up and getting on

CHAPTER ONE

Career progression

Part of understanding the new employment culture is a recognition that career paths and career opportunities are no longer focused on the notion of working up through one organization. The traditional approach to a career suggests starting off in a relatively junior position in some organization and then, through a combination of performance and time serving, working your way up the hierarchy (see Figure 1.1). This approach to a career was probably never a successful or optimal strategy but it did represent a relatively safe option for many people. In the current climate it's still the preferred option for some, but it's certainly not the safe option it once used to be.

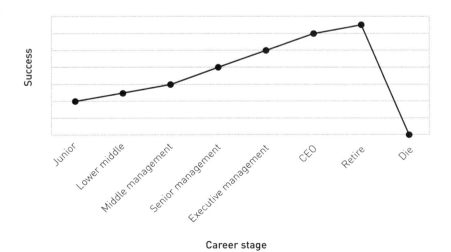

Figure 1.1 The traditional career progression dream

Essentially this model involves the abdication of responsibility for your career progression to the employer – and that can have its drawbacks.

Flaws of single employer career progression

Getting your foot on the bottom rung of the ladder and working your way up was probably never a particularly successful strategy for ambitious people.

Research on progression within organizations suggests that those people who start off higher in the hierarchy tend to go higher and more rapidly compared to those people who start off low in the hierarchy (who tend to stay in relatively lowly positions and for longer). Part of the reason for this can be explained by what I call the 'mums and dads' effect. That is the tendency of your parents to treat you as a child in spite of the evidence before their eyes that you are now an adult. (Well with some obvious exceptions!) In the same way, your boss may still see you are the office girl Friday or the keen young lad. Despite the crows' feet, the peppered hair and the expanding waistline, you are still the officer junior in their eyes!

In an organization if your first impact is as the office junior/teaboy or girl it can be hard to shake off this image in your employer's eyes. This can become a monkey on your back in terms of promotion and increasing your responsibilities.

Another old idea about getting ahead suggested finding a senior manager to act as your mentor. While this is a great idea if you can find one, what happens if they leave or get made redundant? The culture of change that is currently gripping companies means that some can find that their career progression stops when the bosses change and along with it the goalposts shift once more. More sinister is the possibility that you become identified with the old regime and therefore are kept out in the cold by your new boss. Furthermore, value is placed – rightly or wrongly – on breadth of experience before being promoted. Getting broad experience can be an extremely difficult thing to do within one organization. Part of the reason for this is that people have an expectation of moving upwards in the hierarchy rather than moving sideways. The very phrase 'being moved sideways' indicates somebody who is being pushed out of the main game, put to one side, being put out to pasture or into backwater. However, given the high volume of movement within and across organizations, breadth of experience can increase your chances of alternative employment or promotion.

The larger the industry, the more likely it is that your role will be specialized. In smaller firms, all-rounders are common. This means, contrary to the view that large organizations might provide the best career options, it may well be that smaller operations will provide you with a broader training, thus making you more employable.

Modern career paths – a drunken stagger through the world of work

Career paths can more realistically be described as a drunken stagger through the world of work (see Figure 1.2). We are not rational beings and many decisions are made on the basis of a hunch, a feeling or due to unplanned or random circumstances. I call this the 'Notting Hill effect' after the scene in that film when Hugh Grant runs around a corner into Julia Roberts, spills his juice and both their lives change forever! Careers do not always have such romantic twists and turns (although in a recent survey from Griffith University, some 80% of respondents said that they *had*

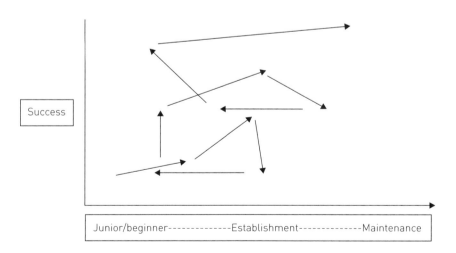

Figure 1.2 The modern career 'path'

experienced office romance), but it does illustrate the point that our careers and lives are not always as planned as we like to think (see Figure 1.3).

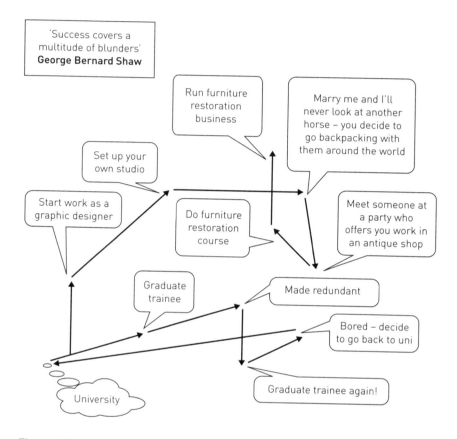

Figure 1.3 An example of how you might stagger through the world of work

Research conducted by the Careers Research Group at the University of New South Wales in Sydney has found that 70% of people in a large sample said their career decisions were influenced by an unplanned or chance event. The events included: an unplanned work relationship, an accident or illness, an unintended exposure to work they liked or didn't like.

CHAPTER TWO

Ways of working and working to find opportunities

Fast track your career: leave!

Career progression can very often best be achieved by leaving your current organization. If you are taking individual responsibility for your career management, then your value should not depend on the arbitrary structures that your organization may have in place or other factors beyond your control. Furthermore it's important to recognize the management trend towards increasingly less hierarchical structures. Much of the 1980s and the 1990s saw middle management jobs being cut out of organizations. Although many might now say this was a bad thing, one of the side-effects of this has been significantly to reduce the career progression opportunities for many people by setting the bar extremely high – you are either at ground level or in the executive suite – the lifts don't stop at many floors in between anymore. In other words, you work at one level and you have to make a leap to get to the next distant level within the organization. Trying to make that leap within your organization can be difficult, for all the reasons given earlier.

The clued-up professional should be seriously considering the possibility of leaving and looking for career progression. We have a whole series of common-sense phrases that you could dredge up against the idea of leaving such as the 'grass is always greener on the other side'. I remember reading that somebody did a PhD on the popular soap opera *Coronation Street* and found that the key theme in the show was this: that anyone who leaves the Street comes to no good (especially if, God forbid, they go to London!). The moral of the tale is you are better off staying than going.

This view is very strongly implanted in our culture and can be found in things such as group membership, social identity and loyalty. Part of the problem is that people come to identify themselves too much with their jobs. Just consider how, when we meet new people, very soon after we get past the names stage, we are enquiring about professions. Equally, it is common to hear things such as 'I have been a big bank person all my life' or 'From my perspective as a teacher. . .'. We refer to our jobs in identifying ourselves all the time. This can lead to great difficulty disentangling these things because it confuses your thinking as regards to whether you should stay or go. You and the job have become almost one and the same. So, you worry, what would you (and the rest of your life) look like if the job were not there. Don't confuse your job and yourself – you are not one and the same thing. (Unless you are a C-grade celebrity famous for being famous – in which the answer to your career is *go*! Now! A long way away!)

If you accept the argument that you should take responsibility for your own career, then you might want to take a few other beliefs on board. The first belief is that you have to appreciate that progression through your organization is merely *one* option for your career progression – there are always alternatives.

The second belief is that it is critically important to ensure that you maintain a profile outside your organization and develop skills to present yourself and market yourself outside that organization to maximize your available opportunities.

The portfolio career

Progressing up the corporate ladder within one organization has to be recognized as only one possible strategy and very often the least optimal strategy that you can pursue in terms of career progression. Nearly all the data on career progressions suggest that the people who rise the most rapidly are those who move on regularly. There is increasing agreement among career professionals that a portfolio career in which you develop a series of different skills, developed from a range of different working environments, provides you with the most marketable career skills. If you analyze the career path of many successful people you see they spend a period of time early on developing skills and moving up the corporate ladder modestly. They move jobs and their career really begins to blossom. I had one client who had spent 18 years with a large multinational going from the bottom rung to a lower middle management role. Then he made the leap and left. In the following six years he moved to four major international firms, each time with a promotion and has ended up in a senior executive management role with double the pay he would have been on had he stayed put.

It is very often the case that you will hear people saying things such as 'I should have done it years ago'; after finally going through with the move and realizing that things are not so bad on the other side.

Alternatives to moving up

The alternatives to moving up within the corporate ladder include:

- moving to a better job in a different organization
- moving to a similar job in a different organization or different sector
- moving into a completely different career path
- putting your career on hold temporarily and either
  - doing some retraining or
  - taking a sabbatical to refresh yourself
- working as a consultant for your organization
- starting up your own business working in a similar area to the one in which you were employed
- setting up your own business working in a different area, perhaps based on another interest or another opportunity which has arisen (e.g. from a family business)
- working as a trainer in the area you are experienced in, taking advantage of your experience and knowledge to train other people.

All these options may be available to any of us on any given day and that is the important thing to remember: the only reason that we are still with the organization is that we choose to be with the organization and we choose to do that on a daily basis. There is no other reason you are there other than that you choose to be there. To say otherwise is to admit that you are help-less. If you start thinking 'I am not in control of my career and I have no options' it is likely to lead very rapidly to feelings of anxiety, frustration, stress and possibly develop into depression. Once you start thinking in that irrational self-limiting fashion the likelihood is that you are going to impede further your chances of doing something constructive to change your cir-cumstances. So reinforce the belief that you are working in your company because you choose to and you could choose *not* to.

Maintain your profile

'80% of success is showing up.'

Woody Allen

We can get into a situation where we treat our career a bit like we might treat our house. That is, we let things go a bit, we don't tidy up and we don't decorate quite as often as we ought to. Then, when someone comes to visit or when they come to buy or inspect the house, you have a mad panic trying to spruce things up and things get stuffed behind the sofa and under the cushions, generally trying to make the whole thing look quite presentable. The overall effect is a bit false and if people look closely they will see all the dirty spots and dust in the corners.

Good strategy in terms of career management recognizes that things could change quite suddenly in your career and you need to be prepared. To maxi-mize your chances of going elsewhere in your career and moving to another company it is important to maintain your career in top condition, which means maintaining a profile. People need to know that you are there. It is a bit like advertising; if you don't advertise your product for sale, generally speaking it is more difficult to sell the product. The alternative to advertis-ing is getting word-of-mouth recommendation and this is where network-ing comes in.

This does not mean that you take out billboard advertisements testifying to your latest fantastic achievements. But it does mean that you work actively to set up regular meetings with people who may assist you in finding work outside your company.

The trouble for many of us is that we get so obsessed in the short term in putting our nose down, butt in the air and getting done the work we have to do, that we simply don't have the energy or the time to think about these other sorts of longer term issue. You often see this sort of behaviour in small businesses. They get a contract and will work flat out to fulfil that contract. Once it comes to an end they find they have no work and no clients, because they have spent all of their time fulfilling that one contract and no time planning and looking for work to put in place once they have finished. This kind of pattern can lead to booms and busts in companies and can cause havoc in terms of their cash flow. The same applies if you don't have some strategies developed in your career. If the decision to leave is forced on you, you are going to find yourself in difficulties. So, if you are made redundant or you are sacked, get shoved sideways, are overlooked for promotion or become sick or injured, you may find yourself in an awkward position and unable to move quickly and effectively. Networking at this stage is less effective and can be counterproductive. You might give off signs of anxiety and desperation in relation to moving on, making you a less attractive proposition. It is much better making those contacts from a position of strength and self-confidence.

Equally, things might change in such a way that you become fed up. There might be a critical moment in your life when you decide to take yourself in hand and change your career path. There may be new relationships or a bereavement. If you have maintained your career, your profile, your network and your career intelligence, you will be in a much better position to be able to make a decision about whether you should stay or leave. Always know:

- what is available
- what the trends are within the industry
- where the opportunities might arise.

Be curious about work and other possibilities

If you start thinking: 'I am going to stay unless I can be convinced otherwise' you will not engage in appropriate exploratory behaviour. You will have a limited network within your industry and none in other appropriate areas. You might possess self-limited beliefs about your transferable skills. You might underestimate your skills, leading to the feeling that you have little to offer another organization. I discuss those issues in chapter 8.

Finally, you might not possess the appropriate vocational knowledge of what you could do with the skills that you do possess. This is a common problem for people who work for long periods of time within fairly narrowly defined jobs. They simply have no conception of what it is like to work in a different environment or what the demands and benefits are of working in those environments.

CHAPTER THREE

Plans, schemes and surfing the waves

'Nothing will ever be attempted if all possible objections must first be overcome.'

Samuel Johnson

In this chapter I am going to introduce some simple but effective techniques that you can use in planning your career transition. The decision of whether you stay or leave is a very difficult one for most people and it can lead to periods of self-doubt and can be an emotional time for many people. Therefore, it is a good idea to have some clear signposts so you can understand and appreciate that you are making progress in your journey to whatever decision you ultimately come to.

Solving your problems

The first approach worth considering is to think about your situation and any problems that need solving. Not convinced that there is a problem? Think of it like this. Write down on a piece of paper: If everything went right in my life over the next two years what would my life be like? On a piece of paper set out work-related issues and personal issues and sketch out if everything went right for you where you would be. Now get another piece of paper, put down the headings 'work' and 'personal' and sketch out where you think you are currently in relation to those ideals. See the example I've completed in Figure 3.1. You can then complete the template in Figure 3.2.

Your current situation			In two years	
Personal	**Professional**		**Personal**	**Professional**
No long-term relationship	Not using skills		Satisfying relationship	Work as a marketing manager
Get fitter	Bored		Lose 10 kgs	Have a range of products to market
Go sailing	Don't like the boss		Go sailing	Work in a team-based culture
Live in a nice area	Not appreciated		Live in a nice area	Have clear sets of performance goals to measure achievements

Figure 3.1   Personal goal setter example

Your current situation			In two years	
Personal	**Professional**		**Personal**	**Professional**

Figure 3.2   Personal goal setter template

Now have a long look at where you are currently and where you want to be in two years' time. How does your life now compare to the one you want to have in two years' time? You may find that there are several areas in your life – both personal and work – you may need to work on. That means you now have some goals!

Getting to your goals

How do you achieve those goals? The first step is to alter your thinking so that your behaviour is aligned with the goals. This means that every time you make a decision that is related to one of the goals you check that what you are about to do will take you closer to that goal.

For instance, if the goal is to get fit, each time you open the fridge door you must run your goal check and ask 'what food can I eat that will satisfy my hunger but will not pile on the kilos?'

Short-term needs that become long-term problems

The main reason people fail in their longer term goals is that they get side-tracked by short-term needs. In relation to work, many people will justify staying with one firm because they know their current job provides the security they need to meet their financial obligations. To move is a risk. So in the short term they are happy because they can pay the rent, the gym sub-scriptions and the rest. However, over time, they become less and less ful-filled because they are trapped in a poor job and are not getting any closer to their goals.

In the same way that you must forgo satisfying the short-term goal of stuff-ing a carton of chocolate ice cream down your throat if you want to meet your longer term goal of losing weight, you may have to sacrifice shorter term needs and desires to achieve your longer term career objective.

Upward goals

Goals should be:
unambiguous
possible
wanted
assessable
refinable
deadline driven

1   Goals must be **unambiguous**. An ambiguous goal would be 'I want nice things to happen to me' – it doesn't give us much of clue what you want. An unambiguous goal would be 'I want to pass my driving test'.

2   Most experts argue that you should set challenging but attainable (**possible**) goals. You can become very demotivated and focused on the distance still remaining between you and your goal if you set impossible goals.

3   They have also got to be goals which are **wanted** and which you can also **assess** to see if you are making progress. Most things you can measure if you think about it. For instance if you said I want to be happier in two years' time, then unpack that statement and say 'How do I want to be happier and in what way'. Do you want to be happier going to work in the morning? Do you want to be happier as a result of interacting with nicer colleagues at work? Do you want to be happier because your contribution at work is recognized by your colleagues or your boss? Do you want to be happier because you are doing work that is contributing to society and helping others achieve more? Do you want to be happier because you are happier with your body shape? Do you want to be happier because you are living in a different suburb or in a different house? So you can unpack the happiness into various dimensions reflecting the difficulty that you may have.

4   Goals should be **refinable**. Many writers on this topic seem to overlook this very important aspect. The world is not a static place. People and things change and it is important for you to be able to assess your goals in the light of new circumstances. If you take the view that a goal is an unbending, unchanging thing, you are running the risk of your think-

ing resembling your view of goals – it too becomes unbending and unchanging. For instance, your initial goal might be to leave the company and find a job with a nicer, more appreciative boss in another company. You start looking and then get phoned one Sunday night to hear that your boss has just been charged by the police for corruption and would you like to take over his job! If you stick to your goal you will lose out on a promotion. If you abandon your goal completely you might find you end up working in the same firm for an even more appalling boss. So you refine the goal by adding to the statement: 'nicer, more appreciative boss, *possibly*, in another company'. You then apply the nice and appreciative test to your potential new boss and if she passes you stay (goal achieved) or you continue to look elsewhere.

5   Goals need **deadlines**. To motivate you, you have to set a date by which time you expect to have achieved the desired change. Without the deadline, you are increasing the risk of prevarication and also of other goals becoming more important in the short term.

Goal travel guide

Figure 3.3 provides a useful tool to help you measure your progress towards your goals.

Work preferences test

My good friend and colleague, Dr Robert Pryor, has an instrument called the Work Aspect Preference Scale, which he uses to measure people's need for different work aspects. These are: money, prestige, autonomy, co-workers, physical activity, security, management, surroundings and self-development. You can see there are many different things that people can want from work and you may find that you are only lacking in a couple of those.

If you have difficulty in breaking it down like that consider putting it on a scale and say to yourself: '1 is the most absolutely appalling thing that could happen where life could become a living nightmare' and 10 would be 'I am absolutely ecstatically happy with my life'. Mark off where you stand on that scale now and perhaps you might even prefer to rate yourself 5 out of

Goals	Personal				Professional			
	Lose 10 kgs		Goal 2		Apply for 5 sales jobs		Increase salary by £100,000	
Deadline	20 weeks				6 weeks		4 years	
	Time Days, weeks, months, years	Progress	Time Days, weeks, months, years	Progress	Time Days, weeks, months, years	Progress	Time Days, weeks, months, years	Progress
	Weeks				Weeks		Years	
Start point	Week 1	95					Year 1	70,00
	Week 3	91						Mid-year promotion £100,000
	Week 6	89						
Mid-point	Week 9	88					Year 2	Review £120,000
	Week 12	87						
	Week 15	87					Year 3	Review £135,000
	Week 18	86						
Goal point	Week 20	85					Year 4	Hit sales target £170,00

Figure 3.3 Goal travel guide

10, about average (see Figure 3.4). By breaking down your goals in terms of knowing where you are on the happiness scale, you can use that to measure your progress towards your goal. This will help you focus and direct your behaviour towards the goals that you have set for yourself. Research shows that this is the most effective way of changing your behaviour.

Use the rating scale (1–10) to answer the following questions.

For each question rate:
A: how important that aspect of work is to you (1 not at all – 10 extremely)
B: the extent to which you have that in your current/recent work
C: the extent to which it would be present in your work in 2 years' time if all went to plan

Example: for question 1, How much independence do you have to do your work your own way?, you might answer: A 9   B 2   C 8

This would indicate that independence is extremely important to you (A), that you have very little at work currently (B), and that you hope to have a lot of it at work in 2 years (C).

	1	2	3	4	5	6	7	8	9	10
	Not at all/none at all							A lot/ Extremely important		
						A	**B**	**C**		
						How important is this to you?	Now or recently	In 2 years' time if all goes to plan		
1	How much independence do you have to do your work your own way (e.g. pace of work, hours, approach)?									
2	How much support do you get from your co-workers (e.g. friendship, practical help, ensuring the job gets done, not letting you down)?									
3	How much have you developed new skills and learned new things (e.g. new skills, tasks, knowledge, procedures)?									
4	To what degree can you be creative in your work (e.g. design new things, develop new approaches, think up solutions)?									
5	How much money and remuneration do you *feel* you get for your work (e.g. salary, bonuses, superannuation, car etc.)?									
6	To what extent does your job provide you with your desired lifestyle (e.g. status, holidays, invitations, where you live)?									

	1	2	3	4	5	6	7	8	9	10
	Not at all/none at all							A lot/ Extremely important		
						A		**B**	**C**	
						How important is this to you?		Now or recently	In 2 years' time if all goes to plan	
7	To what extent are you respected and admired for the work you do (looked up to, envied, acknowledged)?									
8	To what extent does your job allow you to help others or society (help people in need, build a better society, help people lead better lives)?									
9	To what extent is your job secure (certain of keeping your job, certain will always have a job, work will always be available)?									
10	To what extent do you have to manage other people (plan/ arrange others' work, set goals for others, have authority over others)?									
11	To what extent can you get away from your work (e.g. leave it at the office, not get calls outside work, not have to work in your spare time)?									
12	To what extent does your work involve physical activity?									
13	To what extent do you work in pleasant surroundings (location, safety, clean and tidy)?									

Work preferences test results

Aspect	Current dissatiscation	Motivation to change
	Take C from B (C – B)	Multiply current satisfaction score by A A × (C – B)
1 Independence		
2 Co-workers		
3 New skills		
4 Creative		
5 Money and remuneration		
6 Lifestyle		
7 Status		
8 Help others or society		
9 Job security		
10 Management		
11 Work–life balance		
12 Physical activity		
13 Pleasant surroundings		

(Based on the Work Aspects Preference Scale © Congruence 2002 and produced with the permission of Dr Robert Pryor)

Figure 3.4 Work preferences test

Example calculation:

So, in the example given earlier, you answered question 1: A 9, B 2, C 8.

Then you would have C – B: 8 – 2 = 6.

Multiply that answer by A: 9 x 6 = 54.

If you plot this on the chart in Figure 3.5 you would put a cross in the box under the 50 column about halfway across. The mark is clearly in the dark grey area. In the last column in the chart, indicate whether the score is in the dark zone or not. At the bottom there is a 'totals' box for your dark zone scores – the more there are, the more you should consider leaving.

ASPECT	Stay				Go					Is score in the dark zone?
	More likely to stay				More likely to go					
	10	20	30	40	50	60	70	80	90	
1 Independence										
2 Co-workers										
3 New skills										
4 Creative										
5 Money and remuneration										
6 Lifestyle										
7 Status										
8 Help others or society										
9 Job security										
10 Management										
11 Work–Life balance										
12 Physical activity										
13 Pleasant surroundings										

Total number of dark zone scores

Number of scores in the dark zone	Action
2 or less	Definitely stay put in your current job. It is satisfying most of your needs now and into the foreseeable future
3 or 4	Leaving is not the best option in most cases. Look at where the darkest scores fall. Is there anything you or your boss can do to improve these aspects of your work in your current job? Unless those dark score elements are significantly more important to you than other aspects of work, stay and work it out
5 or 6	Leaving is looking like a reasonable possibility. You have significant dissatisfaction across too many areas of your worklife to stay happily. Continuing without the possibility of any improvement is likely to be soul destroying and so you should determine whether improvements can be made in the dark score areas. If not, go!
7 or 8	Leaving is looking like a strong possibility. You feel as though you are missing out on most of the things you look for in a job. Recheck your answers to see if you have been fair to your job. Then consider whether there is any likelihood that the job can be improved enough to satisfy you by raising your concerns with your boss. If not, hit the road, Jack!
9 or more	Leave now! Do not even bother reading the rest of this! You feel as though you are missing out on most or all of the most important aspects of work

Figure 3.5   Work preferences test results chart

Producing checklists is a good way to monitor your progress towards goals. You could set these out quite systematically to produce a series of questions that you need to answer on a regular basis, perhaps giving yourself a score out of 10.

CHAPTER FOUR

Techniques to encourage job exploration

'There is danger in reckless change, but greater danger in blind conservatism.'

Henry George

For many of us, getting ourselves in the right frame of mind to consider leaving actively, and then to start genuinely searching for alternatives can be daunting. You may not even realize that a change of job may be a solution to your problems. Goal setting is a powerful approach for people who are able to articulate to some degree what it is they would like to change about themselves or where it is they would like to go in respect of their career. The trouble is that many of us have great difficulty in articulating that goal and, in addition, many of us don't really know what it is that we like doing. This can lead to many problems with our careers. Generally speaking, emotional factors can play a significant role in influencing our career decisions. Some of the most common client problems encountered by career professionals include:

- No clear idea of what you want to do.
  - If you have never worked or had only negative work experiences you may have little information about the world of work and few definite opinions or beliefs.
- No insight into personal strengths and weaknesses.
  - Some people simply do not know how good they are. I have seen many people doing mundane jobs who, when tested, reveal the intellectual potential for university study and management roles. People who have left school prematurely perhaps due to family circumstance, poor

teaching or simply lack of interest can come to believe they are failures when it comes to training or education and thus avoid situations that may challenge them or otherwise highlight their intellectual capacity. This type of self-limiting behaviour can severely restrict your vocational options.

– If you have little in the way of formal education but find (for instance) that you read frequently and widely or are good at puzzles and crosswords or can find your way rapidly around maps and plans – better than most of your friends – you may be pleasantly surprised at your formally assessed abilities. Get an organizational psychologist to give you a vocational assessment. It could prove to be a great confidence boost and set you looking for jobs you felt were beyond you.

– Others (although this is rarer in my experience) hold the firm conviction that they are a heavenly gift to the world of work in the absence of any supporting evidence such as intellect, temperament or even luck! This can lead to limited career options because they continually apply for unsuitable jobs and get a hefty share of rejection slips. This, in turn, can lead to bitterness and a highly developed sense of unfairness. Neither attribute is an attractive one for potential employers.

- No motivation to explore alternative careers.

  – This is partly what the current volume is all about. Motivation is a complex subject and the reasons for possessing or lacking it are many and various. It can be due to self-defeating talk, lack of confidence, low self-esteem, a low tolerance for ambiguity and the converse – a high need for control, a sense of hopelessness (perhaps developed out of many rejections) or other dysfunctional beliefs.

- Endless prevarication about career planning.

  – Generally, this masks a high level of anxiety about the decision. Occasionally, it can be due to the individual being a poor decision maker. In goal terms, it reflects an obsession with the shorter term needs and not the longer term goals. It can also be an attention-grabbing device – the person plays the role of the victim in a quandary, thus ensuring lots of reassuring and ego-boosting feedback from friends – 'of course you should apply, you are marvellous' etc.

- Unrealistic expectations about what jobs can offer.

- These can be divided into the genuinely unrealistic and the deliberately unrealistic. Some people believe that work can or should offer them nearly all their material and spiritual nourishment. Few jobs (with the possible exception of captain of the Australian cricket team) will provide this level of satisfaction across so broad a set of values. For most this simply reflects a lack of information about the jobs including the pros and cons. The teenage (?) fantasy of being a rock star falls into this category. They don't consider that with opportunities come costs – for instance, the transient lifestyle, the risk of falling victim to capricious public sentiment, the bad haircuts and your friends constantly snorting all your talcum powder in error.

- Some play a sophisticated game with themselves where they deliberately 'expect' work to be able to provide all the bounteous and beautiful things the world can offer. As a consequence they can reject all possibilities as being 'not up to their standards' – a bit like some people looking for Mr Perfect, instead of Mr Right, or even Mr He'll Do!

● Overly modest or self-limiting beliefs about personal abilities.

- This relates to the lack of self-insight mentioned earlier, although it also encompasses people who know how good they are but feel constrained from saying. They are the ones who start application letters with the words 'First of all, may I point out that I do not have the relevant qualifications and experience'.

● Anxiety about change, uncertainty or the unknown.

- Terrorism is terrifying in part because it cannot be wholly predicted when, where or how it will raise its ugly head. We all have a need to be able to predict what is in front of us. The trouble starts when we become intolerant of any uninvited intrusions into our view of the future. In culinary terms, this person would be in the grip of panic if offered the à la carte menu rather than the 'set meal'. A meat and two veg person if there ever was one!

● Inability to focus on the bigger picture or move beyond your current difficulties or issues.

- Problems are irritating little blighters. Like fizzy drinks (with the notable exception of Champagne, of course) once inside you they tend to expand rapidly, making you feel bloated and nauseous. It is easy to become so engaged and enraged with a work problem that you cannot see beyond solutions that involve large amounts of plastic explosive or a heavy blunt kitchen instrument. People who have suffered misfortunes at work such as accidents or redundancy can often focus on their plight to such an extent that they are unable (and sometimes unwilling) to move on and take positive steps for future work.

- Fear of trying out new things – the fear of failure.
  - This is a very common emotion. None of us likes to be humiliated – and I am told by others that it is unpleasant to be wrong. However, while the majority of us can move on or laugh off or otherwise put down to experience any setbacks we have, others become terrified at the thought of failure. They see it in absolute terms and failure means absolute disgrace and shame. I talk about overcoming this in later chapters, but also briefly now.

Fear

Fear is a paralyzing emotion that narrows your mind, thereby reducing the likelihood of your engaging in trial and error behaviour in relation to your career. Exploring new possibilities or working in different ways are really powerful methods to effect change in your worklife and fear can stop these methods in their tracks (see Figure 4.1). This can result in boredom and frustration. The behaviour is often rationalized as the 'stick to what I know' philosophy. It sounds plausible, indeed compelling, until you realize the consequences of such an approach. Alas, the world of work rarely is kind to devotees of the 'do nowt' approach. Jobs, products and customers change regularly and rapidly. This world will not fit neatly and conveniently into the unchanging and highly predictable framework that you have established for yourself. You are essentially setting yourself up for failure.

There is some good news, however! There is a lot that can be done to help you to overcome fear and some of it involves using techniques such as goal setting.

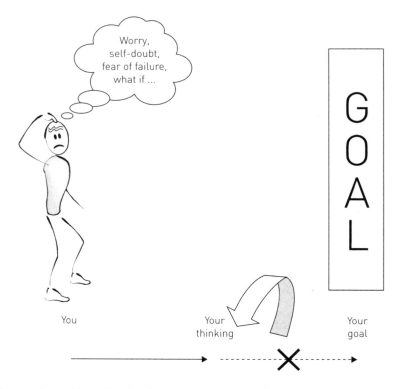

Figure 4.1 Self-limiting thinking prevents you reaching your goals

Crash through or crash

For some people the most effective way of dealing with this is forcing themselves to overcome their fear which can be done either through emotion-focused techniques or through deliberately seeking out new experiences. The emotion-focused technique is just like throwing yourself in the deep end to see if you will sink or swim: in other words, just throwing yourself wholeheartedly into something, suspending your belief and fears and just seeing whether or not you are able to cope in that environment (see Figure 4.2). This approach bypasses all the negative thoughts and any prevarication.

Before you use the crash-through technique you need to consider what environmental constraints there are and whether there are any mitigating circumstances. If there is a genuine and reasonable risk that you could get

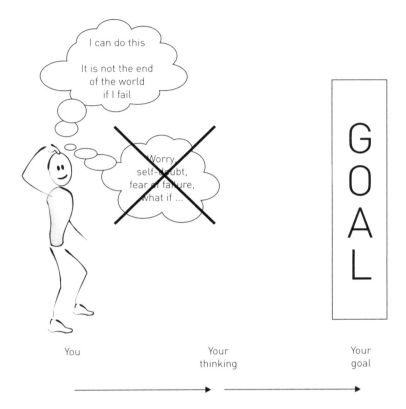

Figure 4.2   Tackle your self-limiting thinking directly to help achieve your goals

fired or hurt yourself or others this needs to be weighed up first. This method can work for some people, but clearly is not something that can be used by everybody.

Chance events

We live in a world in which we are encouraged to believe in a strictly rational view that holds out the promise that all can be explained and predicted and that this is not only possible but desirable. Nearly everything we do in society is driven by this scientific approach. Chance or random events tend to be downplayed and dismissed into the obscurity of the third division – a bit like Leyton Orient. Chance is treated a bit like the rakish uncle who appears tottering up your garden path each Christmas Eve – one not to be trusted with the Christmas sherry. While they are fun, they are still a worry!

Chance factors are increasingly being recognized in the employment area as playing a major role in the decision to stay or go. Work that I have done with Robert Pryor, Sharon Wilkenfeld, Jo Earl and Lene Jensen has indicated that 70% of people indicate that chance factors have influenced their choice of career. Chance events can include unplanned:

- meetings
- new relationships
- experiences at work
- change of address
- injury or illness
- acts of kindness.

Chance events can change the course of people's lives. The 'Notting Hill effect' I mentioned in Chapter 1 is an example of this. You never know whether Julia Roberts is lurking around the next corner waiting to have a romantic interlude! (This is why you will find me hanging around street corners!)

In the movies we recognize that chance events can play a role in our lives. We accept them because implicitly we recognize they *do* happen in life. Some of the negative ones like injury we accept as happening but we don't think it will happen to us.

Injury can have a profound effect on a person's working life. No one plans to get injured. (Although I am not so sure of this having seen what has happened to the English cricket team touring Australia.)

On a more positive note, if you read the autobiographies of successful people it is common to hear of stories of chance meetings, unexpected mentors and unplanned events which apparently played a key role in developing their careers. It is unlikely this can all be put down to modesty.

Capitalizing on chance

‘Serendipity means searching for a needle in a haystack and instead finding a farmer's daughter.’

Anon.

One of the best ways to enhance your career is to embrace chance. Don't treat chance like the black sheep in the family by not talking about it and accepting it. The simplest way to capitalize on chance is to follow the common-sense view – 'you should get out more often'. With the exception of natural disasters and so on, most unexpected events involve other people. Therefore it stands to reason that the more 'other' people you meet, the greater your opportunity to experience a chance event. This is a fancy way of saying 'you should get out more often'. If you are sitting at home on your own watching television there are only two chance events you might have: a meteorite hits your house or you actually find a Eurovision song that is good. That's pretty much it. So going out, or at least joining hands to contact the living (communicating), is the best way to increase your chances of a chance event. Most chance events are caused by other human beings because human beings are frustrating, annoyingly and endearingly unpredictable (see Figure 4.3). It tends to be other people rather than things that create jobs and job opportunities.

Figure 4.3 Capitalizing on chance events

According to the Australian Bureau of Statistics, about 80% of jobs are never advertised in the press. They go to people on word-of-mouth recommendations on the basis of who you know, not what you know. A small portion of these encounters come from chance events: being in the right place at the right time; and knowing the right people. The best thing that you can do is put yourself in the right place. You can never predict if it will be the right time but you can certainly put yourself into places where people know about you. This means putting your name out in different circles. It means embracing an attitude of open mindedness towards opportunities.

Goals are great and you should be working towards them, but at the same time appreciate that life is totally unpredictable and be prepared to revisit and revise your goals in the light of changed circumstances.

Putting yourself about is a method that deliberately invites the unexpected to your house for dinner and a good old chinwag. Here are some suggestions:

- If you go to business conferences, try going to one totally outside your area of interest or expertise. If you are an engineer, go to a human resource conference or a medical conference. If you are a sales and marketing type, try going to a scientific conference.
- Get on the internet and get involved in a discussion group.
- Read as widely as possible – if you never read novels, go to the bookshop or library and have one recommended to you (and then read it). If you read fiction, try a book on chaos theory or physics. (Now there *is* fiction!)
- Join an adult evening class in something new to you – flower arranging, photography, computers, boat maintenance, history, art etc.
- Join a community group or charity.
- Resist the temptation to talk about yourself at parties, but ask everyone you speak to to tell you about themselves.

Even if these activities do not throw up a chance event there are other benefits you might reap including:

- a broadened mind
- flexible thinking

- understanding of other people and groups in society
- new friends and supporters
- increased confidence in your ability to meet new people and try new things
- some amusement and insights from your new learning.

You can't tell me anything

While fear is a major hurdle to overcome when deciding whether to stay or go, another equally problematic frame of mind is arrogance. The know-all is a difficult person to help and they never help themselves. Some of the symptoms of this are that the person:

- will not listen to others' views ('what would they know?')
- assumes they are always correct ('have I ever been wrong before?')
- invents post-hoc rationalizations to cover up mistakes they have made ('well, I know that I should have sent the parcels to London, but I wanted people in Sydney to enjoy the product as well, so I sent them there')
- makes no effort to keep up to date or attend professional development sessions ('oh, that old hat, we did a similar thing four years ago')
- displays a stubborn reluctance to change ('you can't teach an old dog new tricks')
- has a superior, even pompous demeanour.

This form of thinking obscures proper decision making about staying or leaving. The individual has got into delusional thinking believing that they no longer have anything else to learn and they are really at the stage of total domination and mastery. That being the case, they reason, why should they leave? This kind of thinking is often driven by an underlying fear of the unknown. Equally, it can be indicative of someone who fears failing in front of people they consider to be junior/inferior to them. By avoiding taking on new work practices and learning generally they avoid any chance of being made to look foolish. This thinking structure can end up like the fear of failure issue discussed earlier. Such a lofty position means that not only will the individual stall their career, they also risk stalling as human beings. Ultimately, their work becomes repetitive, mundane and boring. They have no room to develop and no room to change. People then can become discordant and be seen to be out of touch, out of date. Of course, they can become a prisoner to their aloof attitude as they are unable to reach out for assistance. Seeking out training or a mentor is seen as a failure of their previous lofty approach. Consequently, such individuals can be condemned to a self-limited and withdrawn, unexciting life.

Retired elite sportspeople can get like this. You can hear it in the comments they make about the game they used to play. They don't appreciate that the game has moved on, they believe it was better in their day and that the modern sport is boring/or less skilful. Such figures are irritating and inadvertently amusing – but don't become one in your own field of work.

PART TWO

Recognizing your situation

In this part of the book, I set out some tips for better understanding the situation you find yourself in. You are clearly experiencing some sense of disquiet about your work and life, perhaps even turmoil. The issue is: how can I reconcile these feelings to the work and non-work parts of my life? Chapter 5 focuses on you and your feelings. Chapter 6 focuses on your job and your employer. You need to understand both as fully as possible to make a good decision.

CHAPTER FIVE

Signs that it is time to leave your job

Personal audit

In this chapter, I set out ways for you to consider warning signs telling you that it is time to leave your job. Very typically, this is a time clouded in emotion because very often we are dissatisfied with our job or unhappy or there may be some interpersonal issues, which are promoting the thoughts of moving elsewhere. Given that emotion comes into this decision so regularly, having a systematic way to appraise your alternatives and to measure the situation that you find yourself in is a great way of ensuring that you are systematic in weighing up all the different factors that contribute to your enjoying your job and ultimately to whether you should stay or go.

There are two aspects to this that need to be considered. The first is *you*. You should do a personal audit to see how you are travelling, to see how you feel about your work, where you see your work going and where you see your life more generally going and the sorts of thing that you might want to do to improve your well-being, some of which will be work related. The second half of the equation is to conduct an organizational analysis. This is to consider where the organization is going, what the opportunities are for you within the organization, where the organization fits more broadly within the industry and industry trends; what sort of people are in the organization, what sort of personnel are in the organization, what are they going to be doing and are they going to help or hinder your career.

The first aspect of this analysis is 'the personal audit' (see Figure 5.1). You need to ask yourself the following sorts of question.

1   'On a scale of 1 to 10 with 1 being miserable and 10 being complete ecstasy and bliss, how happy are you at the moment?' 'On a scale of 1 to 10, how happy would you like to be in a year's time?'

Take away the first score from the second and write down the difference in the box.

2   'How frustrated are you at work now: on a scale of 1 (absolutely, completely and utterly frustrated) through to 10 (totally unfrustrated, happy, content)?' Now ask yourself: 'How frustrated would you like to be in a year's time?'

Take away the first score from the second and write down the difference in the box.

3   'The opportunities to use my skills at work are: 1 (totally non-existent, never use my skills) to 10 (constantly using all my skills and learning new ones).' 'Ideally, how would you be using your skills in a year's time?'

Take away the first score from the second and write down the difference in the box.

4   'In the last three years I have developed new work skills: 1 (not at all, I've stood still or gone backwards) through to 10 (I've learnt extensive new skills at work).' 'Over the next year, how many new skills would you like to learn: 1 (absolutely no skills, I'm quite happy thank you) through to 10 (I would like to develop a whole range of totally new skills).'

Take away the first score from the second and write down the difference in the box.

5   'Over the past three years I have taken on or been assigned significant new work responsibilities, such as supervising others or doing a different aspect of a job: 1 (none at all, absolutely no new responsibilities or even some taken away from me) through to 10 (a whole range of totally new and extensive responsibilities).' 'Over the next year, how many new responsibilities at work would you like to have: 1 (absolutely none at all) through to 10 (extensive new responsibilities)?'

Take away the first score from the second and write down the difference in the box.

6 'I have experienced the following number of significant challenges and problems that I have found motivating to take on and overcome: 1 (absolutely none at all, all the challenges are horrible or no challenges at all) through to 10 (lots of significant motivating challenges).' 'Over the next year how many challenges would you like to have from your work: 1 (absolutely none at all, thank you) through to 10 (lots of challenges, I thrive on them)?'

Take away the first score from the second and write down the difference in the box.

7 'The people I work with are: 1 (my mortal enemies, I can't stand them and they cannot stand me) through to 10 (the best friends that I have ever made in this world).' 'The friends that I would like to have made from work in the next year are: 1 (non-existant, not interested in new friends) through to 10 (the best friends that I have ever made in this world).'

Take away the first score from the second and write down the difference in the box.

8 'The money I earned in my job over the last couple of years has been: 1 (totally pathetic, barely adequate or totally inadequate to keep me in the style to which I'm accustomed) through to 10 (I have money to burn and I like lighting bonfires).' 'Over the next year, how much money would you like to earn from work: 1 (totally pathetic, barely adequate or totally inadequate to keep me in the style to which I'm accustomed) through to 10 (I have money to burn and I like lighting bonfires).'

Take away the first score from the second and write down the difference in the box.

9 'The number of hours that I have put in at work over the last couple of years have been: 1 (almost every living, breathing hour of my life including weekends and evenings) through to 10 (perfectly reasonable and modest hours that don't cause me any difficulty in terms of fatigue).' 'How many hours would you like to be working in the following year: 1 (almost every living, breathing hour of my life including weekends and evenings) through to 10 (perfectly reasonable and modest hours that don't cause me any difficulty in terms of fatigue).'

Take away the first score from the second and write down the difference in the box.

10 'Generally, my boss thinks that I am: 1 (totally ratshit, useless and a waste of space) through to 10 (a crucial and highly valued member of the team who is recognized as a top performer and hard worker).' 'Over the next year, how would you like your boss, in any company, to rate your behaviour: 1 (totally ratshit, useless and a waste of space) through to 10 (a crucial and highly valued member of the team who is recognized as a top performer and hard worker)?'

Take away the first score from the second and write down the difference in the box.

11 'There are some people at work who I really cannot stand and they make all the difference between my enjoying the job and hating it: 1 (absolutely on the money, totally true) through to 10 (absolutely, completely wrong, nothing could be further from the truth).' 'Over the next year, would there be people at work who make all the difference between my enjoying the job and hating it: 1 (absolutely on the money, totally true) through to 10 (absolutely, completely wrong, nothing could be further from the truth)?'

Take away the first score from the second and write down the difference in the box.

Figure 5.1 provides the template for you to fill in. Remember for each question provide a rating for how things are now and how you'd like things to be in one year.

Rate yourself now and how you'd like to be in 1 year's time	Now	1 year's time	Difference
	1 Miserable	5	10 Bliss
1 How happy are you at the moment?			

	1 Totally	5	10 Not at all
2 How frustrated are you at work now?			

	1 Non-existent	5	10 Constant
3 The opportunities to use my skills at work are . . .?			

	1 Gone backwards	5	10 Extensive new skills
4 In the last three years I have developed new work skills . . .?			

	1 Less responsibility	5	10 More responsibility
5 Over the past three years I have taken on or been assigned significant new work responsibilities . . .?			

	1 None	5	10 Lots
6 I have experienced significant challenges and problems that I have found motivating to take on and overcome . . .?			

	1 Enemies	5	10 Best friends
7 The people I work with are my . . .?			

	1 Pathetic	5	10 Heaps
8 The money I earn in my job is . . .?			

Rate yourself now and how you'd like to be in 1 year's time	Now	1 year's time	Difference
	1 Too many	5	10 Just fine
9 The hours that I have put in at work over the last couple of years have been . . .?			
	1 Ratshit	5	10 Highly valued
10 Generally, my boss thinks that I am . . .?			
	1 Totally true	5	10 Totally untrue
11 There are some people at work who I really cannot stand and they make all the difference between my enjoying the job and hating it . . .?			
	Now	**1 year's time**	**Difference**
Totals			

Figure 5.1   Personal audit form

Key

Now score

Score	Meaning
11–33	You are soundly and firmly disaffected in your current role and should seriously consider leaving or making some other changes at work.
34–44	You are mildly disaffected with work, but may have several serious gripes. Can these be resolved at work? If not, consider leaving.
45–66	Look at your individual scores. You either have a mix of things you love and things you hate or work is not that stimulating, but not enough to seriously bother you – watch this carefully and consider how your satisfaction may change over time.

67–88	You seem pretty content overall; leaving doesn't sound that sensible an option.
89–110	Can I have your job? You sound like everything is going fine. Do not consider leaving unless there is some significant other issue.

***Difference** score*

Score	Meaning
0–33	You seem pretty content overall, leaving doesn't sound that sensible an option.
34–44	There are some areas where you would like to see some improvement – you must decide whether these can be either tolerated or overcome, perhaps in discussion with your supervisor.
45–66	There seems to be a significant gap between what you have and what you want. Will your current job evolve to fill these gaps? If not consider leaving when the opportunity arises.
67–99	You are soundly and firmly disaffected in your current role and should seriously consider leaving or making some other changes at work. Are you being realistic in your expectations?

Career plateaux

Another major issue for many people which they need to recognize and should be a factor in their determination of whether they stay or go is the dreaded career plateau. The term 'career plateau' is used to describe that situation where you are no longer climbing the mountain towards the summit. You haven't reached the summit, but you have reached a level at which you have stayed for sometime. Your career has flattened out and you are going neither backwards nor forwards. This is often associated with mid-life crisis, because it tends to come midway through your career when you are halfway up the ladder.

A typical story goes like this. You have:

● gone into an organization

● had some success initially

● been promoted but not for the last five years.

For one reason or another your career has stalled. This may be due to personal reasons. For instance, this stalling process happens very often to women. They reach a certain point and don't get promoted beyond this. Some of the reasons for this are:

- sexism and prejudice generally
- the fact that boys don't want to play with girls
- the woman will insist on going off and having babies and therefore ensuring the future of the planet (which really is terribly selfish, of course!)
- this means they can be out of the workforce for critical periods of their careers, are taken out of the decision-making loop and generally are not to be trusted at all!

For others, it may simply be that they have run out of energy and don't get promoted as circumstances may prevent it. For instance, they may be in a 'dead man's shoes' situation. In other words, they can't move up to the next rung of the ladder until the person on that rung dies (don't even think about it!), resigns or gets promoted themselves. This is something that is seen in very hierarchical organizations, such as the military. The trouble with hierarchy is that the further you get up towards the apex of the triangle, the narrower the range of available jobs, until ultimately there is only one job and therefore each year you get promoted your chances of getting promoted again become progressively slimmer: there are not as many opportunities available to be promoted into.

So what are the signs that indicate that you may be in a career plateau? Well one of them is that you have reached a dead end at work. There is no promotion or prospect of any promotion in the foreseeable future. You find yourself doing the same things and doing them the same way, over and over again. You have a terrible feeling that you have been marking time, as though you are counting down the days until you retire. More likely you are counting down the days until the weekend. You start feeling as though you are living only for the weekend. So what are some of these danger signs in reality?

- Your garden is more interesting than your work.
- The person you trained is now your boss.
- You have not been promoted for five years.

- You are doing the same things in the same ways that you were doing five years ago.
- You don't want promotion even if it is offered.

The last one may seem surprising: you don't *want* promotion even if it is offered. But often this is a good way of looking at your career and seeing that it has stagnated. Believe it or not, many people who are frustrated at work simply do not want to take their bosses' job. They are not frustrated because they haven't got their bosses' job. They actually have come to the realization that the bosses' job is not at all desirable and won't necessarily take them in the direction in which they want to go. This can be a very frustrating situation, because it leaves you with no option other than to stay in the work that you are doing or to move on. If you are happy in the work you are doing it is not a problem, but if you are getting frustrated and bored it suggests strongly that you should move on if everything else, such as available jobs and finances, permit.

Being in a career plateau really is a problem for many people. There is plenty of research that has shown quite a negative and psychological impact on people. One US study showed that people who have plateaued at work were more absent from their work. They also tended to have a poor quality of relationship with their supervisors. In general, they tended to have a lower education and impaired health. This is one of the reasons why I argue very strongly that people maximize their employability and maximize their chances of having transferable skills. It is essential that you keep your skills up to date by doing regular professional development refresher courses and new training. The minute you take the view that you have learnt all there is to know or have learnt all there is that you want to know you are essentially dying and receding from that point. It is very sad when you see these people and we all know of the cases of the trainers and lecturers, politicians, film stars and rock stars, who have gone on just a bit too long such that the material they are producing really hasn't developed or changed. So they are stuck in a sort of time warp for maybe ten or 20 years. The death is slow and painful, nobody wants to tell them, but it happens in thousands of minor humiliations – they are overlooked, not discussed and become increasingly irrelevant. This can happen on a much smaller less public scale with your career.

In a Canadian public service study, the perception of having reached a plateau at work led employees to adopt new behaviours and attitudes. They created a resentment towards their own careers and as a result of that their organizational commitment became weakened. So the people who feel that they have reached a dead end can get angry with themselves about their careers and think: *Well, this is a second rate thing, I am no longer interested in doing this.* The things that increase people's perception that they have reached a plateau include the absence or inadequacies of management practices linked to career planning development and the lack of opportunity to play new roles and participate in work groups. This is where managers have a critical role to play and this is something you need to take into consideration in your current situation and any other potential companies that you will go to. How good is management? Do they have proper career development practices in place? Can they point to evidence of career development in most people rather than in just a few rising stars? Have they got a track record of promoting people or moving people around departments or providing people with new opportunities and challenges? They are questions that you should ask and things you should consider when you carry out your organizational audit.

What are the sort of things you can do to avoid a career plateau? As I have said before, the main one is to seek out further training. Put your hand up for further training. Volunteer for it. Research training on the web. Get yourself put on training circulars, newsletters. Make enquiries about potential training. Ask your colleagues about the training they have been on and how useful it was. Ask people in the areas that you are thinking about going into what background and training they have had and what training they would recommend given your situation. Volunteering for new projects is another way of getting out of the career plateau. The nature of volunteering puts you down as somebody who has the initiative and motivation to help the company. That in itself can be enough for employers and supervisors to recognize that you have done a little bit more than the next person and therefore they may treat you more favourably and offer you more interesting work or projects. The very fact that you are going to be working on a new project is in itself interesting and challenging because it introduces variety into your work.

Time to leave your job: conducting an organizational audit

So now you have conducted your personal audit, you know what is driving you from a personal level. But what about the broader issues? What is going on in the company you are working for and what is going on in the industry and in the world of work more generally? It is important to have some idea about these issues before you make your decision. For instance, you might be very happy with your current situation and on the basis of the personal audit decide that you will stay put. This decision might totally ignore pertinent facts about the organization, such as the fact that it is collapsing faster than an English batting order.

Some of the questions that you might like to ask yourself in relation to that are the following:

- Is the company expanding or retracting?
- Are the glory days of the company over?
- Do customers or clients like the products and services that your company provides?
- Do you agree with your company's philosophy in its general direction?
- Is the industry your employer is in expanding or contracting?
- How good are the opportunities for you to find work outside the company in your local town or city or village?
- Is there a reasonable possibility in the near future of being forced to relocate due to your office, factory or shop closing down?
- How secure do you think your job is, from 1 totally secure, almost impossible to get rid of me through to 10 totally insecure, could be sacked or made redundant on any day?
- What are the chances of getting a meaningful promotion within the company in the next 12 months?
- Would you be likely to receive a redundancy payout if you hung on a bit longer with the company?
- Have you considered asking to be made redundant?
- How good is management?

- Do they have proper career development practices in place?
- Can they point to evidence of career development in most people rather than just in a few rising stars?
- Have they got a track record of promoting people or moving people around departments or providing people with new opportunities and challenges?
- How likely is it that personnel who make your job unpleasant will remain with the firm in the medium term?
- Has the company been through or is it going through a prolonged period of change and restructuring?
- Is the restructuring causing you to question your job?
- Do you know people who have been made redundant in the firm recently?
- Were any redundancies in your area or related to your job?

Other questions that you should ask in relation to the industry are:

- How many competitors are there for promotion?
- Have you got evidence that other people in the company are likely to get ahead faster than you – such as through favouritism or through being particularly strong competitors?
- Is the company prone to a takeover or merger?
- If the company is a takeover target how secure would your job be?
- How attractive is the company's pension scheme?
- How much have you invested in the pension scheme?
- Can you roll over your pension entitlements into another fund?

And some questions about the world in general:

- Is the economy expanding or retracting?
- Do you hear commentators talking about there being a recession?
- Is the level of unemployment relatively high historically?
- Are there increasing numbers of people unemployed?
- Think about your friends and colleagues who live in the same area as you. Of the ones with similar backgrounds and qualifications, how easy

have they found it to find work? How long have they been out of work or between jobs?

● Are similar jobs available in your area?

I have created an organizational audit to assist you in your deliberations (see Figure 5.2).

		Yes/no?	Score 1 for yes; 0 for no
1	Is the company retracting ?		
2	Are the glory days of the company over?		
3	Do customers or clients dislike the products and services that your company provides?		
4	Do you disagree with your company's philosophy in general direction?		
5	Is the industry your employer is in contracting?		
6	Are the opportunities good for you to find work outside the company in your local town, city or village?		
7	Is there a reasonable possibility in the near future of being forced to relocate due to your office, factory or shop closing down?		
8	Is your job at risk?		
9	Do you think you will not be promoted in the next year?		
10	Would you be unlikely to receive a better redundancy payout if you hung on a bit longer with the company?		
11	Have you considered asking to be made redundant?		
12	Are the management members poor?		
13	Do they have poor career development practices?		
14	Do they focus only on nurturing a few rising stars?		
15	Has your job stayed pretty much the same for a long time?		
16	Are all the unpleasant staff likely to remain?		
17	Has the company been through or is it going through a prolonged period of change and restructuring?		
18	Is the restructuring causing you to question your job?		

19	Do you know people who have been made redundant in the firm recently?		
20	Were any redundancies in your area or related to your job?		
21	Are there many competitors for promotion?		
22	Have you got evidence that other people in the company are likely to get ahead faster than you, such as through favouritism or through being particularly strong competitors?		
23	Is the company prone to a takeover or merger?		
24	If the company is a takeover target, is your job insecure?		
25	Is the company's pension scheme poor?		
26	Have you invested little in the pension scheme?		
27	Can you roll over your pension entitlements into another fund?		
28	Is the economy expanding?		
29	Do you hear commentators talking about there being a jobs boom?		
30	Is the level of unemployment relatively low historically?		
31	Are there decreasing numbers of unemployed people?		
32	Think about your friends and colleagues who live in the same area as you. Of the ones with similar backgrounds and qualifications, have they found it easy to get work recently?		
33	Are similar jobs available in your area?		
Total number of yeses			

Figure 5.2 Organizational audit form

Key

Points	Meaning
0–7	Either your company is in good shape or you believe it is. If you are convinced of the accuracy of your answers, then leaving doesn't sound the right option here. Compare this score with your personal audit. If your audit also says stay – that

sounds like the end of it. If the audit says go, consider that the problem might be an interpersonal one, or your own motivation – sounds like the company is doing its bit for you.

8–15   Check to see whether your yes responses were mainly for general things or for the company specifically. If they were mainly company problems, there are perhaps enough of them to consider leaving. Bear in mind that no company is going to score brilliantly on all measures and you should go back and consider your answers carefully before deciding what to do.

16–24   The company sounds in poor shape. If there are plenty of available jobs, consider leaving, but check the personal audit first.

25–33   Sounds like the company is stuffed, your job is under threat and there are opportunities outside. Look back at your personal audit. If that suggests you should go, this is SCREAMING GO!!

CHAPTER SIX

Signs that it is time to stay put

Sometimes it is easier to identify reasons to leave than it is to find reasons to stay. Often people stay out of habit, familiarity or because they have never thought to leave. However, it is worth seriously thinking through why staying is a good idea. If you *have* gone through this process it may reduce the chances of your becoming resentful in later years, when you do decide to go, because you have left it too long. You will be able to point to a series of valid reasons why you stayed.

Some signs that it is better to stay than leave include:

- poor job market
- poor state of the economy
- recent promotion/track history of promotion
- rock solid promise of new position /promotion
- excessive personal debt
- not been with the company long enough
- been through several jobs this year already
- no job to go to
- no idea of what other work you could do
- somebody in a position you aspire to is strongly rumoured to be leaving
- the idiot you report to is strongly rumoured to be leaving
- the working conditions mean a lot to you and are unlikely to be replicated elsewhere (e.g. personal freedom, childcare, holiday allowance, pension scheme).

Poor job market

You don't want to leave a job if your chances of getting another are very poor. This can depend on the state of the job market. Predicting the job market can be as tricky as spotting a black cat in a darkroom. Many things influence the job market and some are very hard to spot. In the late 1990s every man and his budgie were trying to get into internet companies. People were almost throwing money at people who worked in the industry. Some companies (such as mining firms) found that they could raise more money by floating an internet company on the stock market than they could from their established businesses. Then investors woke up to themselves, sold their shares and the industry went into a drop that approached terminal velocity. One month this was a great industry to work in and only the next people were falling over themselves to get out of it. A similar thing happened in the information technology and telecommunications industry.

The best way to assess how an industry is faring is to read the business press on a regular basis and watch current affairs and business programmes on TV. It is also worth scanning the internet for stories on the industry.

Labour market fluctuations can be a local issue too, such as a company pulling out of a local town. It can be further localized to your company struggling financially. Conversely, as the epicentre of the impact gets closer to you, the harder it can be to find out what is happening. It is a bit like being in the eye of a storm. Information can be gleaned from colleagues and supervisors. The questions should be asked in such a way so as not to arouse suspicion or to alert people to your motives. Rather, the questions should be framed as showing a responsible and motivated interest in how 'we are all travelling'. Also, of course, the source of all true information in a company are the secretaries. They usually have a fair idea of what is happening because they have the ear of the key decision makers, plus they see lots of strategic documents.

Some individuals and firms specialize in collecting labour market information such as salary rates, employment prospects and training availability and requirements. Try searching the internet under 'labour market data' – you might get lucky.

Poor state of the economy

This is closely related to the state of the labour market. The state of the economy mainly impacts on you in terms of how it affects the prevailing business climate for your industry. It can also have a direct effect in terms of mortgage interest rates. At the time of writing interest rates are at the lowest levels seen in 40 years. However, only ten or so years ago they were approaching 20% (or four times today's levels). Variation in rates could have a huge impact on your personal circumstances. If you suddenly need significantly more money to pay the mortgage, leaving work and risking a period without paid employment becomes a much less attractive proposition. Equally, this can also lead to belt tightening in companies, meaning fewer job opportunities.

While many of these things are large-scale effects, there can be significant variation by industry. So in a time of war, the leisure and air transport business can be in recession, but the armaments industry experiences rapid growth. While taking the economy into account, it is better to focus first and foremost on your circumstances and those of your employer.

Recent promotion/track history of promotion

If you have recently been promoted or enjoyed a track record of promotions then it suggests you are highly regarded and doing well within the organization. These are generally potent reasons to stay and any decision to leave should be very carefully evaluated. What chances are there you will continue the upward path in a new setting? What is it about your current work environment that allows you to perform so well and will these elements truly be in place elsewhere?

Sometimes the promotion can be a stepping stone to elsewhere, however, you should be sure the 'elsewhere' is truly a place you want to be. Equally, your latest promotion might have been unequivocally your last (i.e. there is simply nowhere left for you to go within the organization).

Rock solid promise of new position/promotion

The key words here, without a doubt, are 'rock' and 'solid'. So many careers are stalled by people waiting on promises that do not eventuate that you should be wary of going down this path. I learned this lesson early in life from my 'colourful' Uncle Jack. He was a second-hand car dealer at that stage in his life and he offered the young Jim a ride in a Rolls-Royce that had turned up at his garage. I waited all Sunday afternoon at the end of our drive for him to turn up – he never showed. All Sunday afternoon seems like a lifetime to a young lad. 'Rock solid' promises have some of the following properties:

- They have a time limit.
- They have a clear and unambiguous payoff.
- They have clear and unambiguous conditions that are measurable objectively or by mutual agreement that can be checked.
- They are in writing or an email.
- They are made by people who unequivocally have the power and discretion to make them.
- The only extenuating circumstances to break them are like what you find on insurance policies (i.e. acts of god, war, famine, pestilence).

If your 'promise' does not have at least three of these features, relying on it is extremely risky. As a very crude guide, if all six applied, then waiting six or so years for the payoff may be worthwhile; then deduct a year for each feature your promise lacks.

Excessive personal debt

If your finances are stretched to the limit and a bit beyond, moving jobs is a much greater risk. For instance, if you have a huge mortgage and your credit cards have reached the end of the line, you have little room to move financially and any relatively trivial impost could send you over the edge. Clearly, if the new job pays more then it can be a very good (and very common) move. However, the issues to consider here are:

- Does the increased remuneration come at the expense of job security?
- Is the increased remuneration linked to performance bonuses or sales targets and, if so, how attainable are they?
- Is the job subject to an initial probation period and, if so, what is the realistic expectation that you will get through it?
- Are there significant costs associated with taking the new job, such as buying new work attire, purchasing travel tickets, a more reliable vehicle or the necessity to use personal credit cards to cover reimbursable expenses such as overnight accommodation?

Not been with the company long enough/been through several jobs this year already

Unless the position you are thinking of moving into is absolutely bang on the money and the materialization of a vocational dream, moving around with indecent haste is often a big career mistake. While you may be able to get into another job immediately, it could be the one after that where the problem starts. For by then you could have three or four jobs within 12 months to explain on your résumé. Moving around like that leads employers to make negative attributions such as unreliable; immature; unlikeable; on the make; unsure what they want.

No job to go to

Assuming you need to work for a living and you do not have significant cash reserves to draw on, this option should not be considered unless there are overwhelming extenuating circumstances. It would need to be some very serious problem at work or elsewhere in your life to do this. For instance, a very serious illness affecting you or a loved one; or a very serious issue at work such as harassment that you have been unable to deal with satisfactorily in other ways. Generally, it is easier to find work if you are in a job than if you are not.

No idea of what other work you could do

If you do not have a clear understanding of what else you could do for a living or lack knowledge of what is available that matches your skills and abilities, then you risk moving into an another job that closely resembles your current one and (assuming your current disaffection is more than people issues) you will run up against the same issues again. Go and see an organizational psychologist and get a vocational assessment done.

Somebody in a position you aspire to is strongly rumoured to be leaving/the idiot you report to is strongly rumoured to be leaving

First, check if the rumour is true. Go and ask Elvis (because he *is* still alive) or the astronauts who didn't really land on the moon. If you work on the basis of discounting 90% of office rumours you will be wrong, typically, on no more than 10% of occasions (but you may have to watch more soap operas to make up for the loss of dramatic intrigue in your life!). If the rumour has some credibility (and most of what I said about verifying a promise earlier stands here) then consider hanging on a *little* longer.

The working conditions mean a lot to you and are unlikely to be replicated elsewhere

It is possible in your ruminations about leaving that some aspect of work has become the focus or flashpoint for you. For instance, you may have convinced yourself you are underpaid (try convincing yourself you are overpaid – funny how this is so much harder to do . . .). Often we get disillusioned because we make inappropriate social comparisons. We pick people who we feel are our equals for some arbitrary reason such as their age, their qualifications, their experience, the time spent with the company, where they live etc. We then focus on points of difference between them and us – generally, those points that show us in the poor light. However, we often fail to take into account the points of difference where we have the better deal. For instance, we look at our mate and see they earn 20% more than we do. We get irritated. However, what we don't look at is that you have a rostered day off each month (so that equals 5% extra), you also have a pension plan where the employer puts in an extra 7% (now the differential between you and your mate is 8%). Finally, you can walk to work in five minutes and she has to drive for up to one hour. Take into account the costs of travel and the loss of two hours of her time each day and you are probably nosing in front. Then add on the free after-hours childcare facility and the staff discount card and you are looking like Bill Gates compared to a church mouse. Do you really want to give that up for a little bit of lousy (taxable) money in your pocket? Wake up to yourself!

The stay–go decision, contract work and renewals

When it is time for renewal of a contract many of us are compelled to consider alternative employment. It is not uncommon for people who know that their contract is about to expire without any clear indication of a renewal in the offing to start actively considering leaving a company. This is often one of the reasons why people talk publicly of the possibility of leaving. Very often this is a form of defence mechanism. You want to get in there first and make it look like your decision to leave and not management's. This threat to leave is often just a cover-up, a screen for the anxiety you feel about the possible threat of job loss (and accompanying self-perceived loss of dignity).

It is advisable not to broadcast broadly and widely that you are thinking of leaving. The people who need to know that you are thinking of leaving include potential competitor organizations, other potential employers and people who are in significant position of influence who may be able to introduce you to others who have work opportunities. In other words, none of the people in that list includes your workmates! Your workmates generally should not be told about these sorts of deliberation because this could undermine your position within the company if they see an opportunity arising from your departure. Certainly do *not* tell your supervisors.

Never suggest to a supervisor that you are actively thinking of leaving, unless you are genuinely thinking of leaving and are prepared to carry it out. You don't want them to call your bluff. In one example I can think of along these lines, an individual said to a newly appointed manager: *'If I don't get a pay rise I am going to be leaving.'* The individual thought that the new manager would be a soft touch. He was absolutely horrified when this manager called him back into the office and asked him what sort of leaving present he would like to have and for when should it be arranged. Ultimately, that person did end up leaving the job, but not on his terms. His bluff had been well and truly called. So don't advertise your thoughts along these lines. It is like teenagers and sex: very often the ones that talk about it the most are the ones who have yet to go through with it!

As more people move into fixed-term contract employment as opposed to permanent positions, it stands to reason that more people than ever do not have their contracts renewed. This can increase the likelihood of people entertaining thoughts of leaving, sometimes motivated by the fear of not having their contract renewed. There is no shame in not having your contract renewed, it happens to many good people. Contracts can reduce employee commitment because they become distracted worrying about their job security. Not only can people find it very stressful due to the uncertainty, many long-serving or senior staff can find the process extremely insulting. I can think of a good colleague with an excellent work record who nonetheless is obliged to work under the contract system and actually took a demotion down two rungs on the ladder to go to a competing institution that offered some tenure of employment. She got thoroughly fed up with the games that were played in the contract renewal process. Negotiations were endlessly put off, endlessly drawn out and with no firm commitments being offered at any stage. Eventually, she had had enough of it and procured herself a place somewhere else. Of course, at this stage her old employer suddenly rushed through a renewal of contract offer, but it was too late (despite being a good offer). By that stage she had already made the psychological commitment to move elsewhere because of the shabby treatment.

So the contract renewal period is a high danger point in terms of the leave–go decision and it can sometimes provoke people into leaving perhaps unnecessarily or under circumstances in which they would not normally do so.

CHAPTER SEVEN

Money matters

The stay–go decision often has a financial component to it and even if this is not your primary motivation or interest it pays to look at your financial situation and the financial implications of any move seriously. One of the issues facing baby boomers is that they have spent so many years on the Chardonnay, the Bolly and generally going for it, they haven't considered the longer term financial implications of saving for what are fast approaching retirements. Money is one of those things that can either fascinate us endlessly or be about as interesting as watching Geoff Boycott make a well-compiled 12 not out before lunch at Derby on a freezing April morning. Whatever your take on this, either get actively interested in the financial implications of your decision or, preferably, get appropriate expert financial advice. What follows is an organizational psychologist's outline of some of the issues – but this should not be seen as replacing proper financial advice from the appropriate experts.

Know your entitlements and benefits

The sorts of thing that you might receive at work include:

- salary (a quaint custom that most employers would probably like to do away with if they could)
- superannuation – old-age pension paid to you when you retire: from a private fund perhaps in addition to a government pension
- share-options:
  - profit share
  - share save
  - company share option plans

- – share incentive plans
- – enterprise management incentive schemes
- – long-term incentive plans
- – other company schemes
- company car
- school fees
- health plan
- in-house legal advice/conveyancing
- reduced interest personal loans and mortgages
- sporting facilities
- workplace nurseries and crèches
- luncheon vouchers
- relocation expenses
- long service awards
- loan of company computers
- company-sponsored education and training
- insurances – life, death and accident, loss of income, professional indemnity
- accommodation
- subscriptions – magazines, clubs, professional societies
- discounted goods and services.

Pensions or superannuation

Many people have no idea that they have money in their name sitting in little superannuation accounts around the place. While you might have relatively small amounts of money tied up in such schemes, if that money is 'rolled over' into one account, over time it could amount to a significant sum. Very broadly speaking, there are two forms of superannuation scheme that are relevant to most of us. In one scheme, you get a defined benefit on retirement that is linked typically to your average salary in years immediately before you retire. These schemes pay out regardless of the investment performance of the fund and is the responsibility of the employer to pick up any shortfalls. Not surprisingly, these schemes are on the way out, mainly I suspect, because they pose too great a financial risk on the employer (and are too generous in the employer's view). In such schemes, should you leave early, a benefit amount is calculated using actuarial principles. The way this is calculated can be very complex. Many people feel that they lose out in such schemes by leaving before retirement and certainly, if you are very close to retirement, this might be a serious consideration. (Go get some financial advice.)

Increasingly common are the investment schemes where money is paid (from your contributions and/or your employers) into a bigger pool of money that, in turn, gets invested in financial markets. Your payout is dependent on the performance of the fund. It is generally easier to move in and out of such funds and the calculation of the worth of your benefit amount (the amount you can take with you when you leave to reinvest in another pension scheme) is less opaque.

Superannuation as a topic is enough to get the worst insomniac asleep in seconds, but it is worth persevering with, because the amounts of money involved could be considerable. It is also the most likely form of non-salary benefit that you will receive at work. It is a highly complex field and I want to recommend no more than you should bear it in mind in your deliberations. Superschemes or pension plans vary and there are different laws and regulations that cover what you can do with the money and when you can access it. Equally, there are rules governing leaving the scheme and what happens to your money. At the very least enquire of your supervisor whether there is a company plan and how to contact the people who run it. If you work for a large company make a point of discussing your pension plans with somebody from the HR department. (Incidentally do not make the mistake of believing that HR people are there to help you – they are there to help management, so do not reveal why you are looking into your pension.)

Cars, loans and the like

You may enjoy the benefits of a car, a loan, perhaps various forms of insurance and so on. It is likely that many of these sorts of thing would cease on your leaving. However, they do not always have to and it is sometimes possible to negotiate for some benefits to extend beyond your employment with the firm. This is especially the case for senior people or if you have been made redundant. Bear in mind, too, there is no reason why you cannot make an offer to buy things such as your car or company computer. Equally, you could negotiate to take over responsibility for a club membership or get your employer formally to nominate and second you if appropriate.

Incentive schemes, bonuses and shares

There is a large and profitable industry out there devoted to finding new ways to manage the exchange of your labour for some form of reward. These schemes can be as complex and require the same finetuning as a Formula 1 motor car (and, in some cases, the dough involved is about the same!). Suffice to say, before you flounce out of the door, work out whether you will get a bonus under the company preferential, mutual, totalizer, round-the-houses, in a brown envelope behind the bike sheds, offshore, equity-based, deep-pan, cheese-crust incentive scheme.

Also consider the value of any shares that you may hold in the company. If the company is not publicly listed you may not have a good idea of the value of the shares. In some cases people are given these 'shares' as a gesture. The shares are not meant to be traded or cashed in, but provide some decision-making power for the individual concerned – they have a stake in the company. When it is time to leave they can get a nasty surprise at the worth of these.

Bonuses, golden hellos and parachutes

Equally, it is possible to lose out on bonuses if you leave at the wrong time. If your company has year-end bonuses and you leave in November, you might not be entitled to anything at all. It could cost you thousands. If you are in that position and you have lined up a very enthusiastic suitor, you should be considering negotiating a 'golden hello'. This is a payment or bonus on joining the firm which might compensate you for lost entitlements or equally for any relocation or upheaval you might experience. You could also ask for an equity stake as well if you have had to give one up in your previous role. Equally, you might be in a position to negotiate a golden parachute – benefits and payments on leaving. Although it sounds strange to get these for leaving (although not in my case!) – it can be seen as a reward for a job well done or as compensation for loss of future expectations – a bit like a redundancy payout. This all needs looking into carefully before you take the step through the exit door.

You can see from this very cursory consideration that financial aspects of the stay–go decision can get surprisingly complex very quickly and if you are in a position where you are subject to one or more of these schemes or arrangements, it is essential you calculate the financial implications both of staying and of going.

PART THREE

Mind games

In this part, I address some of the tricks we can play on ourselves by thinking in unproductive ways about our dilemmas. The way in which we think about a problem can have a profound effect on the solutions we generate and the way we subsequently behave. Problems can be tackled from many different perspectives and not all are going to help you solve the problem. Look at this picture, for instance. Which is higher up, A or B?

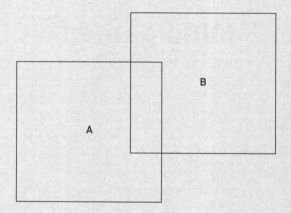

It could be B because it is higher up the page. Equally, it could be B because the square it is in is actually sitting above the square A is in. Equally, it could be A because it is sitting in the square above B! Finally, they could be on the same level if A and B marked the sides of a cube! It depends how you look at it.

CHAPTER EIGHT

Recognizing and conquering self-limiting talk

'No one can make you feel inferior without your consent.'

Eleanor Roosevelt

Perhaps the most common dilemma we all face when considering whether to stay or go is winning the battle of the emotions. What I mean by this is working through and getting clarity among all of the competing thoughts and feelings, anxieties, worries and concerns and all the anger, frustration and threats.

We can construct equally 'valid' views of whether to stay or go that are absolutely logical and internally consistent but clearly contradictory.

Overthinking

One of the major problems that people have in this area is called 'over-thinking'. That is, endlessly to churn through the dos and the don'ts, the ifs and the buts, the maybes and the what ifs. Continually looking for the pluses and the minuses of any situation or course of action, in the mistaken belief that by doing so you will find some ultimate clear answer and an obvious path of action. This is extremely misleading and I've yet to hear of anyone who has gone through the extensive agonizing of staying or leaving who has come to a rational or comfortable decision on the basis of doing that.

One of the reasons that we engage in all this agonizing, internalizing and ruminating is the cultural value placed on the undesirability of making up your mind very quickly. We have lots of expressions in the English language that reflect this. People who do so are seen as superficial, shallow, irrational, illogical, cavalier, impetuous, wilful, headstrong or stubborn. Similarly, expressions of common sense such as 'Fools rush in where angels fear to tread' and 'Less haste, more speed' also point to the social undesirability of making up your mind quickly.

While it is undeniably true that people do make mistakes and take wrong turns and they do this as much with their careers as with anything else, I have yet to see any evidence that people who do make their career decisions rapidly make any poorer decisions than those people who ruminate over them. So why do we do all tend to ruminate like this?

Part of the reason is an aversion to risk. The other part of the reason is a need to have control over ourselves and our destiny, including our careers. We are programmed from birth to be cautious of and stressed by uncertainty. Uncertainty by definition means a situation in which we don't know how to respond. We don't know what is going to happen and therefore we don't know how we should behave. If we don't know what is going to happen it is very hard for us to prepare. This uncertainty leads to stress as one response and people become stressed because, essentially, they get on the defensive and are constantly alert to the possibilities that something negative may happen to them. In terms of occupational stress, the perception of having little control over how we work tends to be associated with feelings of stress far more often than feeling we have too many demands placed on us.

The uncertainty associated with career change decisions is more hypothetical in the sense that the choice 'shall I stay or shall I go' is one that you have to take actively, it is not something outside your control. Of course, this is where the problem lies. Because deciding in the affirmative that you will leave is essentially putting yourself into a situation of uncertainty and therefore quite systematically and deliberately exposing yourself to stress. 'Better the devil you know' is another piece of common sense that tends to speak against taking undue risks or chances.

For several reasons we haven't got our risk and challenge meters properly calibrated. Most of us tend to think that doing nothing is, in fact, the safest possible option. In fact, a colleague, Fiona Jones, who does research on

exercise and health at the University of Leeds has often described my attitude to exercise (where I say that the safest thing you can do at any one
moment is to sit still and do absolutely nothing) as my 'fat bastard' hypoth-
esis! It is quite true that the safest thing you can do at any one moment is
to sit quietly in a chair and relax. Of course, what this misses is the fact that
if you take a longer timeframe, sitting in a chair and generally living a seden-
tary lifestyle is significantly increasing your risk of a variety of negative
health-related outcomes, such as weight gain and damage to the cardiovas-
cular system among other things. Therefore, sitting in a chair doing nothing can actually be a very risky thing to do. It just depends on what your
timeframe is.

Self-limiting talk

For some folks there is a tendency to think:

**‘No I shall stay put, I won't do anything rash and I won't put myself in
a stressful situation because I don't want to cope with the stress. Yes,
my job is frustrating, yes, I get fed up, yes, I don't get on with my boss,
yes, I come home stressed, yes, I work long hours and I am not
recognized. All of that, but, it could be worse if I go somewhere else.
And therefore, unless things get unbearably toxic I am not going to
take that chance.’**

This is what I term as self-limiting talk. The speaker is so afraid about
events outside their control, they place strict limits on what they can do.
They have convinced themselves it is better to put up with an unhappy situation than to explore other possibilities. Such an approach is tantamount
to accepting failure. In doing so they are building a very small safety zone
around themselves and denying any room for trial and error behaviour in
relation to their career. The chances are this person might have this kind of
attitude towards a whole range of other things that they do (and deny
themselves) in their life as well.

This approach to careers is taking a really short-term view and, unfortunately, it is people who tend to think along those lines who can often
become the more tragic cases further down the track when their careers

have stalled. They haven't moved, they've stayed in the same job and, essentially, they've been treading water and have been overlooked by people in their organization. They are seen as lacking in dynamism, ambition and initiative. This dawns on them after a considerable period of time – perhaps when they start seeing the people they trained go onto bigger things – such as becoming their boss. Sadly, such people may have left it too late to make the move and become increasingly stressed and despondent.

The reason that this can be stressful is that we tend to make social comparisons. We tend to compare ourselves with somebody else. In the world of work we very often compare ourselves to people who started work at the same time, people who have worked in the same department or people with similar qualifications. So, of course, everything is going fine while your position relative to those other people doesn't change. If those people you compare yourself to seem to have got on further or become more successful than you it can trigger a period of self-reflection. While you were complacently doing nothing to manage your career actively they were busily beavering away, working very hard to set themselves some goals and taking opportunities as and when they came up.

By the time you find this out and see 'your equals' in their new positions of seniority, time may be running out for you to do anything about it. Then you may end up making decisions based on resentment and jealousy. It is easy to be driven by such negative emotions rather than the more positive values related to developing yourself as an individual, such as taking more responsibility, doing more interesting work and getting some variation into your life.

This may sound as if I am suggesting that people should always take opportunities and move on whenever they are presented. It is true to say that I do have reasonable sympathy with that view, certainly in comparison to the alternative, which is never to take opportunities. If I had to choose between taking the opportunities or never taking them, I would have to go with always taking opportunities.

Get the correct perspective

You should not be thinking about how you are going to be feeling the next week or next couple of months when deciding on your career. Rather, you should ask how you are going to feel in a few years' time and how you are going to feel in ten years' time. A useful exercise to gain perspective is to imagine you are looking back on your career at your retirement party. Say to yourself: 'OK I am now 65, just retired and home from my last day at work':

- How do I feel about my career?
- What sort of things have I done with my career?
- What sort of things have I achieved in my life?
- How have I spent my working life?
- Have I done useful things?
- Has work lived up to its reputation for me?
- Have I got the most I could out of work and what more could I get out?
- How would I have done things differently?

Looking back in this way or looking forward to looking back in that way can be quite useful in helping you to understand your goals and motivations. It also helps you drag your view of risk out of the short to medium term to the longer term. When you start looking at decisions in that context you can see that staying in the same place is a risk (as is leaving), but at least you have made a deliberate attempt to consider the implications of your decision on your career and life as a whole.

There will always be another bus along soon

Treating opportunities in a cavalier fashion and not appreciating their true worth is a great danger and trap for the unwary. One way in which this can happen is when an unnecessarily distant leaving date is nominated (e.g. I will have left in five years). In reality this resolution gets modified to: 'I will not leave in the near future, but I will think seriously about it as the five-year deadline approaches.' This is a comforting self-delusion because you kid yourself you have made up your mind ('I am a decisive person – I have made the decision') while at the same time conveniently putting off any serious consideration of resolving the stay–go dilemma. In such self-deluding situations, as each opportunity presents itself over that five-year period, you will knock it back, rationalizing each rejection by fooling yourself that the 'timing was wrong', 'there could be a better opportunity and so best to wait for that'. After five years you are still in the same job, still doing the same thing and still conveniently swatting away opportunities like pesky flies. Wasting your career always waiting for better opportunities to come along.

Good things can be well camouflaged

This leads into another problem with looking at opportunities. That is the tendency to think that when the opportunity comes which is right for me, I will instantly know it (and take it). Outside of the movies, that kind of immediate and obvious fit between yourself and the job is very rare to find. Indeed, some people would suggest that if these things come so readily and easily to you they are ultimately not going to be satisfying. Some researchers looking at the motivational effects of goals and rewards would argue that the more satisfying jobs are the ones where you truly have to put in some effort and in return you get some rewards. If work is all about reward without effort, so the argument goes, you will tend to disregard it, you'll tend to think less of what you are doing and you won't grow as an individual. You will take less pride in your work. The most unattractive opportunities initially may end up being the most rewarding in the longer term.

In a lovely study some psychologists invented a stupid task which was to read out a public lecture which was total and utter gobbledegook (it was not one of mine. . . it wasn't. . . truly!). It was absolute rubbish, it didn't mean anything and was of no value whatsoever (on second thoughts, it might have been one of mine!). Anyway, they had this lecture and persuaded two different groups of people to give the lecture. To one group of people they said: 'Give this lecture. It is important that this crucial message gets across to the audience. Really give it your best shot.' To the other group of people they said: 'Look we know that this is rubbish but we have been asked to have someone present it. We shall pay you some money to do it.' What they found afterwards is that they asked each group how they felt about presenting the material after they had done it. The group that had done it because they thought it was important typically said: 'I really think this is important, I believe in it and that's why I got involved in doing the work.' Those who got paid some money, turned around and said: 'Oh it's a lot of rubbish but I did it for the money!' In other words, doing things that come very easily and have no inherent value where it's all about reward often leads to the work being dismissed. If you do work that you think is stupid this can lead to longer term reflections on yourself: 'Hey I must be stupid doing stupid work all my life.' This can lead to people having a lack of self-worth: 'What am I doing on this planet? What is my contribution to society?' Consequently, work that involves a happy marriage of effort with reward and inherent interest will ultimately be the best job.

Unrealistic expectations

Another mistake is setting the barrier so high or so unrealistically that all opportunities are rejected because they don't provide all that you want on a plate with no effort on your behalf.

It's a bit like somebody who really wants to lose some weight saying: I will only go on a diet when I can find one that guarantees that I don't have to do anything at all and the weight will just fall off me. The likelihood of that ever happening is remote. It is the same with work opportunities. The idea that the only good opportunities are ones where all your needs are fully and immediately met is unrealistic and self-limiting. Few opportunities will ever pass that test.

Liferaft opportunities

If you start seeing the next job as a liferaft that gets you away from the sinking ship, it probably means that you have left your stay–go decision far too late in the piece. Clearly, there are some unfortunate souls who work for companies that collapse rapidly or suddenly announce out of the blue mergers or redundancies, however, for the vast majority of us that's not what will happen. We have to make decisions, not have them made for us. Now is as good a time as any to start that decision-making process.

Panic now!

Did you know what Joyce from accounts is saying? She was told by Bob from sales that Dave in marketing had spoken to Doreen in HR who said that Morgan in catering was speaking to Matilda in despatch who overheard Gertrude relating to Stan that she was told by the man on the Clapham bus that the company is going to retrench three-quarters of the company in the next few weeks!

It is very easy to set your thinking on a rapid trajectory to the wrong conclusions. For instance, if I were to show you the monthly sales figures in the top graph in Figure 8.1, what would you think? Time to get out of the company. However, taking a different perspective, the bottom graph shows sales actually increasing on an annual basis in what is clearly a seasonal business (Christmas cracker sales in this case).

There must be 50 ways to love your leaver

Don't you just love those cheery coves who, having announced they are quitting, go on to point out that you should do likewise because the company is going down the pan! In a very public act of convincing themselves that their decision was the right one (and betraying their serious self-doubts) they test their (nearly always weakly held) view that the company is shot by trying to convince others. If other sane people can be convinced, then they can feel more confident they are doing the right thing.

Overcoming self-limiting thinking

Recognizing self-limiting ideas and self-limiting talk is the first step in overcoming these negative frames of mind. Some common examples of apparently innocent or well-intentioned thoughts that follow on closer inspection, could be unduly constraining your thinking.

The mysterious 'it' monster

Saying things such as 'It has got to be a great opportunity before I leave' sounds innocent enough, but buried in that statement is a suggestion that

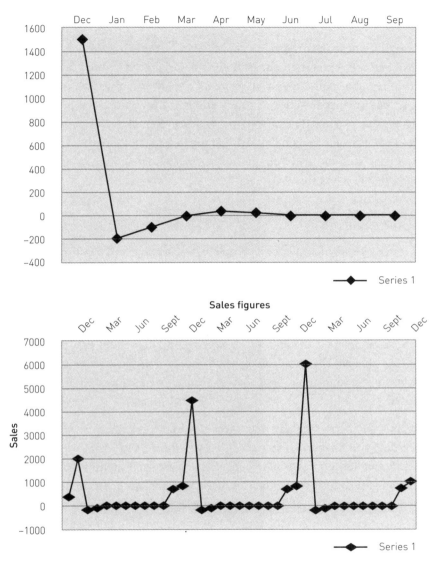

Figure 8.1 Sales figures for a seasonal business

you are the passive witness who is presented with opportunities. What exactly is the 'it' in that statement? A more self-empowering statement would be: 'I would like to seek out a great opportunity so I can leave' – this implies some positive action on your behalf; it is an *active* not a *passive* statement.

Mustabatory thoughts

Albert Ellis describes the tendency to preface thoughts with 'I must' as 'mustabation'! A common one is: 'I must be convinced before I move to my next job.' What is the 'must' in there all about? What do you mean, you 'must' be convinced? Why are you putting that pressure on yourself? The only person placing this burden on yourself is *you*! A better sentiment would be: 'It would be good to feel that moving to another job is the appropriate next step for me.' You are not setting up demanding or impossible standards by saying this.

Now or never

'If I move jobs it will either be a complete disaster or it will be the best thing I ever did.' This is black and white thinking. It is either going to be one thing or another. First, most things in life simply don't fall so neatly into those two categories. It is highly unlikely when you move that your job is either absolutely the best thing you will ever have in the world or for that matter a complete disaster and the worse thing that could ever happen to you. The chances that your job turns out like that are so remote it is simply not worth thinking about. So get away from this 'absolutes' thing. It is not realistic.

Second, it is highly unlikely that a job is going to provide you with all the emotional and financial sustenance that you desire, but equally it is highly unlikely that it is going to fail to deliver in at least some areas. Whatever you do it is highly unlikely to be the end of the world in any sense whatsoever. It may just be a bit of a cul de sac you go down! But ultimately, so what? You have experienced something! You have learned something more about yourself in terms of the work that you like or the work that you don't like. You may well have picked up some new skills or insights and some new contacts or maybe some new friends along the way. Is it really, ultimately that bad?

Fear of failure and comfort from the familiar

Fear of failure in the context of contemplating a new job is the lack of self-esteem and self-efficacy that leads to the belief that you simply will not be up to the job that you are considering moving to. If you have been doing your own job very well and have been with the same company for a few years, you know the system inside out. You may, indeed, have designed the systems in the first place. You could be absolutely familiar with how things run in your firm. This new job prospect may mean:

- taking on more responsibility
- supervising other people for the first time in your life
- using a new computer program
- trying a new process or selling a new product
- working in a different town or country.

This is the recipe for an extremely threatening situation. All those nasty failure questions come to mind:

- What if I can't do it?
- What if I make a fool of myself?
- What if I fail?

This self-limiting thinking works against your seizing the opportunity. Consider the 'What if I fail?' for instance. Well, what evidence is there you are going to fail? Who *says* you are going to fail? Have you regularly failed at things in the past? And if you have failed, what was the outcome? What went wrong when you did fail? You may have experienced some discomfort or embarrassment. None the less you are still here, you have lived another day, you may have found another job. Often things move on and it is not the end of the world.

Another way of overcoming such thoughts in relation to your career is to think about the people around you. If you must entertain thoughts of catastrophe, be aware there are hierarchies of catastrophe! If you really believe something outrageously bad may happen at work, then why not at home too? Think about your partner, your husband or your wife. Think about your children, your parents, your close friends. What is more important to you? Something terrible happening to them or something terrible happening in your career?

Often when people do actually experience a traumatic event – perhaps a close shave with death or a health scare – they tend to get a new perspective on life. It can bring home the realization that today just could be your last day, so why am I worrying so much about things that are beyond my control? Keeping that thought in mind is a way of getting some much needed perspective on these decisions, which should take some of the pressure off you.

That absolute pressure of thinking in terms of succeeding or failing with nothing in between is unnecessary, unproductive and unrealistic. The reality is, that in most cases, it always falls in between these extremes and, consequently, it is a case of perhaps experiencing *some degree* of happiness, sadness or disappointment. If you can take away the pressure and remove some of the emotion in the situations you are half way to making a better quality decision.

Self-limiting talk is an amazingly powerful determinant of our behaviour. It does not reflect reality. It is just a series of beliefs that both restrict you and reduce the chances of your experiencing new things.

CHAPTER NINE

Promises, delusions and head in the sand syndrome

'The advantage of emotions is that they lead us astray.'

Oscar Wilde, *The Picture of Dorian Gray*

This chapter is all about deluding yourself. The previous chapter was all about deluding yourself by defeating yourself before you even start. So this chapter deals with the opposite problem, that is, the one of kidding yourself that there is going to be a positive outcome or that you have skills and attributes which are perhaps an exaggeration of the true picture. Unlike the self-talk, this is something that often involves other people. One of the characteristics and one of the things that most of us, if not all of us, are absolute suckers for is *flattery*. Most of us simply cannot resist hearing something positive about ourselves. This is one reason why horoscopes are so popular. When was the last time you had a horoscope which said: *'Your star sign is herpes and 2% of you are going to die this year.'* They don't say that sort of thing because people simply don't want to hear negative things like that. The one prediction that astrologists could make with a fantastic degree of certainty is that we are all going to die. But, unfortunately, death doesn't sell that part of the newspaper. It may sell on the front pages, but not on the horoscopes page. So, instead we content ourselves with tales of fortune, self-development, romantic encounters and increased happiness. We fall for it, time and time again.

Seduction is an age-old routine (that, in terms of routines, makes Ken Dodd look positively avant garde) which is effective in different areas of our lives and includes careers and jobs. One of the most dangerous traps that you can fall into is of being seduced by promises from others of advancement or perhaps promises of a position. Many careers have foundered on the rocks where people have waited patiently for their turn, having been told and tapped on the shoulder that when the time comes and the person dies or retires, the job will indeed be theirs. Of course, when the event comes around you are overlooked, the position goes to somebody else, an outsider, a son of the boss or some bullshit excuse is given for your not being the right material or, worse still, being dammed with faint praise: 'You are doing such a fantastic job in your current area we couldn't possibly afford to lose you to management.' Very often people who are suffering these delusions and false promises have foregone other opportunities or indeed have given up looking for alternative possibilities and opportunities. The moment the person gives up looking for those alternative opportunities they are being held to ransom by time and by their current employer.

These days it is a really high-risk strategy not to be actively looking around at the job market on a fairly regular basis, if only to find out how in demand your skills are to give yourself a more confident position from which to bargain for a pay rise. You should be regularly appraising the market and the opportunity in that market. It doesn't harm you to have fairly regular meetings with people and explore the possibilities of what might be on offer should you be interested in moving.

Promises from friends and strangers

Promises from other people can come from within the organization and this is fairly common. You bide your time, keep your head down, keep your nose clean and you'll get all the spoils, the promotion and riches and you too will have 'my lovely office at some point in the future'. Of course, many such people are subsequently disappointed.

Equally, it has to be said, these promises can come from outside the company and, in some respect, these promises are even more dangerous and potentially more likely to fall through. The typical line is: 'Come and work for us and we shall give you this and that, and we'll give you a bonus, better car, more holidays, more responsibility', blah blah blah. 'Anytime you want to leave just give us a call and you can come and join our company.' This kind of comment is dangerous because very typically it is made by people who have absolutely nothing to lose by making it. They are not actually offering you a specific job, starting on a specific time and day and so. They are merely generally trying to keep their hand in with you and perhaps trying to impress you with their generosity. They may just want to impress you generally that their company is going places and people like you would fit into it. It doesn't necessarily mean they have a position. If you are not convinced, when you next get offers like that and you are sure you don't want to go to that company, just try gently winding up the person who makes the offer by saying: 'Sure I'll come to your company, when do you want me to start . . . 9am Monday morning?' Then watch their face absolutely drop when they think that you are taking them seriously! I guarantee that 90% of them will be backpeddling furiously!

Giving a gift horse a full dental check

So, if promises are coming from outside the company you need to take some steps to try and establish whether or not they are merely empty promises or whether they are, in fact, a serious approach. Rather than beating around the bush, ask them straight out. Say:

1 I appreciate your interest and it's very flattering for you to suggest that I might have a role with you.

2 How are things going in your firm?

Then you put the next questions hypothetically. You say:

3 Well, supposing I were interested in leaving when would you be looking at recruiting people and what sort of duties would you have in mind for somebody with my skills and experience?

4 What would you envisage my doing?

5 Is this something you would be wanting me to do immediately or something you want me to do should your plans with your business work out in a year's time?

6 Is this something I should be talking to you about seriously now or is this something perhaps we should just keep in touch about over the next 12 months?

If you put the questions like this, you are not saying give me a job and give it to me now. You are not threatening that person, you are not encouraging them make an immediate decision which almost certainly would be a negative one for you. What you are doing is merely establishing the groundwork to talk further seriously about the issues in the short term or just to talk regularly over the longer term. If the person says they would love to have you on board, but it's not quite the right time, that's a face saver for them. It's a face saver for you, too, you now understand that their promises are neither genuine nor serious at this stage. It is just a case of watch this space.

Equally, if the person is serious but didn't want to make an out and out offer then you have set the groundwork and you have given them an indication that you could be interested. The door is still ajar for you to meet again when circumstances change or indeed you could suggest setting a time to meet again in the future if you want to apply some gentle pressure. So always check out promises.

Up yourself!

The second problem can be falling into delusionary thoughts about your own abilities. One of the dangers here is in believing your own press releases (previous CVs). While it's a very sensible tip to keep your CV up to date and to keep a pantry of achievements which you regularly update, the danger is that you review this list of achievements on such a regular basis that you begin to start really believing that you are something extra-ordinary in terms of work! Clearly, it's excellent to be confident in your abilities and confident in your achievements, but, before you jump ship realistically assess your chances in the job market.

You have to back yourself. However, that self-confidence can be taken too far and we can become hubristic. At this point you are really at risk. If you are starting to believe that you are God's gift to the world of employment then you have clearly gone far too far. There are some cultural issues in relation to this as well. Certainly in some contexts, such as within the UK recruitment market and also in the Australian recruitment market, the negative sentiment associated with those viewed as being a 'tall poppy' or 'up yourself' is quite strong and can be counterproductive. While my research shows that blowing your own trumpet is a successful thing to do when applying for jobs, the cultural pressure to refrain from doing so is also quite strong. In other cultures, not only is the social pressure to avoid boasting very strong, it is also reflected in the labour market. There are several common delusions. I set some of the more common ones below.

Whatever you do at work you are fireproof and you will never lose your job

Well, that one can be disproved with alarming haste with accompanying shock and adjustment problems when you are fired!. Equally, it can be the delusion that you are the boss's favourite and you are marked down for the fast track: you're the one who is going to get promoted. And again the impact of that not coming to pass can be damaging to the individual and it can take a long time to recover from that blow. It can also manifest itself in terms of people trying to go for totally unrealistic promotions maybe two or three levels above where they are at the moment. Again, while ambition is commendable, foolhardy and reckless assessments of situations are likely to backfire. For instance, going for senior jobs from where you currently are too quickly or going for the job after being in a company for an indecently short period of time can be seen as arrogant. It can be interpreted as your lacking an appreciation of the complexities of the position to which you aspire. The incumbent in such a job may act like a gatekeeper and be on the selection panel. They are not likely to take well to the idea of some upstart getting into such a position in record time when it has taken them many years of careful career management and achievement to get there.

The delusion of greatness can also get in the way of your continual profes-sional development. You may start to say: 'I now know everything I need to know, I am the expert in this area. I don't learn, I teach.' When people get into that state they start stagnating as individuals and their skills don't con-tinue to develop in the way they should.

I am not liked or I am/will be loved at another organization

Getting into the mentality that either the employees in your current job do not like you or, equally, that people at another company absolutely love you and really want you to go and work for them can be another form of delusion. Feeling you are not liked or appreciated is unpleasant and is often a sign of occupational stress. While the reasons for believing this statement can be well founded on evidence, quite often it can be a sign of oversensitivity or a mismatch between your needs and management's style. While the issue certainly needs addressing, leaving the organization may not necessarily be part of the solution. Look to other issues such as teamwork, interpersonal style, extenuating circumstances (such as periods of heavy work demands). Also, consider whether you were popular in previous organizations. If not, consider working on your own interpersonal skills rather than blaming the job.

Believing you would be popular and welcome elsewhere may be a sign you have succumbed to another's flattery. This can often happen when colleagues have made the aforesaid empty promises, perhaps at some social event, and then you have followed up on those things, assuming therefore that you have been headhunted, when it was merely somebody who was trying to be encouraging or trying to boost your confidence. Alternatively, people can hold such beliefs as a form of coping strategy, i.e. while nobody here seems to like me, I know I would be liked if I went to the other organization.

Believing the rumours

Another sort of delusion that can cause difficulty is believing rumours in office places. One of the most common and destructive rumours that are bound within the office place is: This department, this section, this company is about to close down. Or this department, section or company is about to make redundancies or is losing money. It's a regular and self-defeating rumour that is rampant in just about all workplaces to some degree. This, of course, can lead people to jump before they are pushed and might be doing so on a completely irrational basis. If all companies closed down, went bankrupt or sacked people at a frequency with which the rumours set in, then turnover in organizations and companies would be massively increased and decreased respectively.

Head in the sand syndrome

This is the stubborn refusal to acknowledge events going on around you or acknowledging that it is time to go. This is a very common illusion among elite sporting people, like cricketers who go on far too long so that their batting average suffers! They personally cannot see any decline in their performance. They don't *want* to see any decline in their performance and they become progressively more ambitious as they become overlooked for selection. The head in the sand syndrome is really saying: 'I'm not listening, I don't want to see anything, I am not prepared to take on board what you are telling me or what is going on around me.' Again, this is dangerous in terms of the decision to stay or go because it is getting into a fixed way of thinking. It means set views that are not altered by any evidence. Head in the sand syndrome is a disaster when it comes to career management decisions such as staying or going.

The Welsh delusion

The Welsh song, 'The green green grass of home', is a call to come back or stay put. I suppose Wales must be the other side because 'the grass is always greener on the other side'. It is easy for us to romanticize distant or far off possibilities. We may be contemptuous of the familiar and yearn for some far-off land. However, you are about as likely to find this dream place as you are to find Munchkins and the Wicked Witch of the East (actually, I have a few contenders for that position on my shortlist!).

Some of the questions you should ask yourself to see if you are suffering from head in the sand syndrome are:

- Do you find yourself refusing to believe what other people say about work?
- When was the last time you challenged your views about your job and your workplace: (a) yesterday (b) six months ago (c) two years ago?
- How much of your opinion about your work has changed over the last couple of years: (a) totally (b) a little (c) none at all?
- Do you know all the words to 'Men of Harlech'?

The danger of promises, delusions and head in the sand syndrome is a tendency for you to jump too quickly without having fully appraised the opportunity. It is a bit like buying a timeshare or an apartment off the plan. The promises are made that it is full of fantastic opportunities, the conditions would be brilliant, you will regret it for the rest of your life if you don't take it. Then, of course, you turn up, the timeshare hasn't been built, the water has not been connected, the expected tenants don't materialize, you can't actually see the sea, the weather is absolutely terrible and, in fact, they are going to be building a major international airport at the bottom of the garden. This is what it can be like with careers. You have to ask yourself, why do they need *you*? And what is it they will ask you to do? One of the most common reasons that people will get approached or made promises to is that somebody wants them to replicate what they have done in their current job. In other words, somebody has spotted and seen that the candidate has been a really high achiever in their current work and therefore would like them to do the same thing for their organization. This is all very well and flattering and works very well in careers where you don't expect much in career progression. For instance, professional football players make their money by being good at a particularly narrow set of skills which they can repeat ad nauseum. The trouble is that, with most of us, our careers are not as simple as that and we don't get as much satisfaction from doing the same thing over and over again.

Consequently, one of the reasons we move jobs is to develop new skills or have an opportunity to work in different sorts of job. Even if you have been promoted or been given a fancier title you have got to really weigh up whether or not the work you will be doing will be the same as you are doing at the moment or, worse still, you might go back and have to build something else up.

Builders and maintainers

People can be crudely divided into two types when it comes to their careers. (Did you know that there are two types of psychologist – those who divide people into two groups all the time and those who do not; and I hate the former!) There are the builders and there are the maintainers. The builders are people who like to take new challenges and create something from where nothing existed before. They want a big empty space or blank canvass to work on so they can create big shiny edifices and wonderful creations. They want to be able to point to their creation and say 'I built that' (the *Titanic* or the Millennium Dome!). Try my builders' and maintainers' quiz (Figure 9.1) to see which category you fall into.

1	Do you prefer seeing the big picture rather than the minute details?	not at all absolutely 1 2 3 4 5 6 7 8 9 10
2	Do you get frustrated doing the same thing repeatedly?	not at all absolutely 1 2 3 4 5 6 7 8 9 10
3	Do you see beauty in perfectly arranged, infinitely repeating patterns?	not at all absolutely 1 2 3 4 5 6 7 8 9 10
4	Do you like to be able to point to new things and say that you developed them?	not at all absolutely 1 2 3 4 5 6 7 8 9 10
5	Are you interested in the conservation and preservation of heritage items?	not at all absolutely 1 2 3 4 5 6 7 8 9 10
6	Do you enjoy keeping things running smoothly?	not at all absolutely 1 2 3 4 5 6 7 8 9 10
7	Do you like clear processes and instructions?	not at all absolutely 1 2 3 4 5 6 7 8 9 10
8	Do you enjoy inventing new things or approaches?	not at all absolutely 1 2 3 4 5 6 7 8 9 10
9	Are you comfortable with uncertainty?	not at all absolutely 1 2 3 4 5 6 7 8 9 10
10	Do you enjoy doing administrative tasks?	not at all absolutely 1 2 3 4 5 6 7 8 9 10

Figure 9.1   Builders' and maintainers' quiz

Key

1 Add up your scores by writing the number you circled for each question in the boxes. Then add up each row to get a total.

Q1	+ Q2	+ Q4	+ Q8	+ Q9	**Total** builder

+ Q3	+ Q5	+ Q6	+ Q7	+ Q10	**Total** maintainer

2 Now subtract your **maintainer** total from your **builder total**, add 45 to the result and write the answer in the overall score box.

Total builder		**Overall score**
Total maintainer	–	
	=	+45	
	=	

3 Now look up what it means!

Overall score	Meaning
0–20	You are a strong maintainer, you like order, process and keeping things going.
21–45	You like routine and order, but can deal with change reasonably successfully.
46–69	You have building tendencies, but can cope with routine admin if necessary.
70–90	You are a strong builder, happy with chaos and confusion, eschewing routine and what you see as mundane process.

Builders are fantastic innovators, they are great at solving problems and are highly motivated by the need to achieve something tangible. The downside for the builders is that once you have built the building and once you have laid the last sod of turf and done all the landscaping around the building there is nothing much more for you to do. If there are no new challenges to occupy you, you can become bored and restless.

This is where the other sort of person comes in – the maintainer. Maintainers are people who are not driven by the need to build something brand new. They don't need to identify themselves with the construction of new approaches and they don't necessarily look for challenges at the obvious level. Maintainers are much more likely to find their challenge in keeping something going well, avoiding trouble, elongating the life of something. Keeping things in immaculate condition, restoring things. Such people will gain much more satisfaction out of smaller scale, detailed things, winning a hundred small battles rather than one major war. They are really quite different people. The maintainer will look at you blankly if you give them a greenfield site and if they do anything at all, they might mow the lawn! The builder will build a fantastic building on the site but give them an existing building to look after and very soon the paint will start peeling, the tiles will start falling off and they will almost yearn for the whole thing to fall down so they can start over again. Or they may even get into destructive behaviour by knocking it down so they do have something to build up again!

Therefore, when you are moving jobs you want to have some idea as to whether you are a builder or a maintainer to ensure a match to the new job. One of the dangers is for someone who is a builder to get a promotion to another role which although similar differs crucially in that maintenance is the most important element. Putting the builder into that role can be extremely boring and stressful and is not likely to be productive or successful for either party. A maintainer may have a fantastic reputation for keeping a programme going at the forefront and doing it efficiently, profitably and meticulously. Then along comes somebody starting up a new competing organization. They see this person who is associated with the highly successful existing product and think they can build their competing product to the same level. The mistake is to confuse building and maintenance. That person may have absolutely no skills in relation to doing the building and they may find such a position daunting and one where they would expend excessive nervous energy and stress in achieving the results. Ask yourself are you being asked to build something from afresh or are you being asked merely to maintain things in a smooth way?

10
CHAPTER TEN

Worries and doubts

The decision whether to stay or go is shrouded in emotion and those emotions tend to centre, at the negative end of the spectrum, on having worries and doubts. It is an agonizing decision. We never can be sure that we are correct. We often try to be as correct as we can in our decision and that is the most sensible thing to do. But what we sometimes don't realize is that very often there is no way of telling whether you were correct until a long time after the decision. Even then you can't really tell.

Hindsight is a smug bastard

Suppose you moved jobs and it turns out you are less happy after moving. We may tend to think of the move as a mistake and regret our decision. But what is to say that you would have been much happier had you stayed in your old job over that same period of time? It may be that your old job would have changed or you have become generally increasingly frustrated in life and therefore you would have been no more happy staying in that job than you were in your new one. So although you are not happy now it doesn't follow that you would have been happy staying where you were before. We tend to get into that way of thinking and we also tend conveniently to forget, especially when we make errors, what it was that drove us to that choice in the first place. We tend to diminish the importance of the facts that we weighed so heavily then with the benefit of hindsight.

The main thing about worries and doubts is that any decision in life usually is accompanied by some degree of worrying and some degree of doubt. This reflects the fact that whatever we do in life is to some degree outside our control and we simply cannot predict the future, however much we wish to do so. None of us knows when we go to work each day whether we shall come home that evening. This is not a complaint that is associated just with Bob Newhart's driving instructor. Life is a risky business and there are always decisions to take and there are always going to be relatively unplanned chance events such as accidents.

The worry triangle

Will I be happy?

This, perhaps, is the ultimate worry that drives all the others (see Figure 10.1). It is an intangible thing and pops up in the most unexpected places. Rephrasing the question as why would I be *unhappy*? might assist you in gaining some perspective and realizing that it is just a job, one source among many wellsprings of happiness. Do not beat yourself up looking for absolute guarantees in this department, because the people that make and sell the product called life offer no guarantees other than death and taxes.

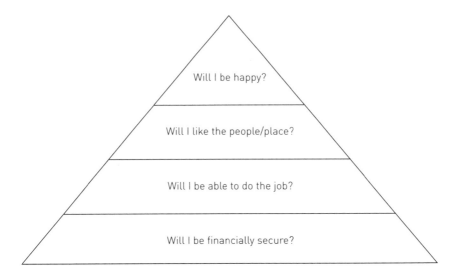

Figure 10.1 The worry triangle

The more insight you can muster, the more likely you will be able to make a fairly accurate stab at this question. Equally, the more you know about the prospective job, the better position you'll be in to answer it. Really, this is one of the underlying goals of this book as a whole: to maximize your chances of happiness by optimizing your decision.

Will I like the people or place?

These doubts include:

- What if I don't get on with the people?
- How am I going to ensure that I *do* get on with people?
- What is it I can do to try my best to get on with people?

You could list some strategies, for instance:

- Make an attempt to remember everyone's name.
- Make an attempt to draw out a map of the office and put the names of people in the various different rooms so you get to know the names of everybody.
- Use first names. This is an extremely powerful way of developing their trust and their friendship.

In other words, look for solutions to your problems. If you are having worries and doubts say, ok, let's pan this out, how would I deal with that situation if it occurred in the workplace and what would be a good solution to that? What could I do if that happens? So, instead of merely throwing your hands up in despair, you take a proactive approach and say, yes, there are some potential threats in this position, there are in anything in life, like breathing, but I think I have thought out ways in which I can handle most of those things and I am going to commit myself to this for 12 months and see how it goes. And if it doesn't go right, well, that's not a problem, all of us make mistakes and after 12 months if things don't work out, I shall review the situation and I can move on.

If this move results in moving to a new state or country there may be issues in relation to how well you fit in. Social questions about not only getting on with your colleagues at work and having a social life, but how you will fit into your new surroundings generally. If you have a family then this concern extends to them. Will my partner fit into this new surrounding, and will my partner be able to support me in my new job and vice versa? Will my children settle into a new school or kindergarten? (Or, for hassled parents, will my children be able to discover my new address!)

There is a whole range of different issues here which can cause people genuine problems and should be addressed. For instance, partners who move between counties, interstate or internationally can catch a condition called *trailing spouse phenomenon*. This is where one partner has decided to comprise their career in the interest of the other and follows that person across the map for their job. Now the person who has got the new job is generally well looked after. Companies these days are very good at accommodating relocated employees, getting them acclimatized, assisting them with visa applications, finding homes, setting up bank accounts and generally introducing them to people in the area, putting on welcoming receptions and so on. So therefore people moving long distances can often have very agreeable processes to help them settle as quickly as possible. Also, of course, they have the challenge of their new job which will be absorbing for them and keep them very much focused on the immediate issues of doing the job well. The trouble is that the trailing spouse doesn't always get the same degree of attention or the same degree of assistance. If the trailing spouse is not working full time then it may well be that they are spending long periods of time at home, they are on their own, they have no support people, there is no obvious way of meeting other people. It can be extremely isolating and frustrating. People who have difficulties acclimatizing may find even the smallest differences in the way things are done from the old country/county/state extremely upsetting. It merely serves to remind them they are not at home. Even simple things like telephone directory enquiries are different, can't find the news or weather on TV, not knowing the radio stations and so on can create potent homesickness and can play heavily on the mind of the trailing spouse.

These things can be overcome, people travel all the time, people move from town to town, country to country, state to state on a regular basis and do so highly successfully and many people thoroughly enjoy the opportunity that they have to work in different surroundings. So although these things are worth considering and taken seriously they shouldn't be things that completely overshadow your decision making.

Will I be able to do the job?

You got it, didn't you? Self-doubt about ability from time to time is normal and healthy. It can motivate us to undertake further training and professional development. Bear in mind, that unless you have bragged your way into the job with outrageous lies and exaggerations, if it turns out you cannot do the job, part of the blame falls on the company that recruited you. They should have spotted these shortcomings during recruitment or they should have understood better the demands of the job they had on offer.

The sorts of worry include:

- Will I be able to succeed in this new job?
- Will I know what I am doing?
- Can I take on this new chance?
- Will I be able to manage people?

Recognize when you are having those thoughts. If you have been recruited to the position or you have been offered another position then clearly the employer is showing confidence in your ability to do the job or at the very least you can say to yourself that the market is so short of qualified people you will be competent in the area or at least able to do most of what they require. Recognize when you move into a new position that you will take a while to get established and before you start working at full efficiency. You also need to think about the fact that you have done this before in the past when you started your first job or perhaps your last job. You managed to establish yourself, you managed to make a success of what you are doing. You managed to hold down a job and you managed to procure several pay rises and success with the organization. So there is no reason why you cannot do that again in the future. Past behaviour is the best predictor of future behaviour in most circumstances.

Will I be financially secure?

This can be a potent worry for all of us and it can never be resolved completely to anyone's satisfaction. As I have already pointed out, research on well-being has shown that those with highly developed needs for financial wealth are often a less happy bunch than those less materialistic. How much is enough? What does security really mean? That you have enough money such that you will never want for anything ever again? That you have enough to pay the school fees and mortgage? As a general rule, increased remuneration goes hand in hand with increased entrepreneurial activity. In other words the bigger the gamble (less security) the bigger the payoff.

Overcoming worries and doubts

One of the ways of tackling worries and doubts is to say to yourself that whatever decision you make it is not necessarily going to be forever. This is one of the hardest things that many of us find when we are moving from one job to another especially when it involves moving address as well is the parting from good friends and possibly families. This can be very difficult to do. However in my case, I made the move from the UK to Australia; it was an extremely significant move for me to leave behind all my friends and all my family. It was a very hard decision to make and it took some time to settle in. I was very fortunate that I had some very supportive family colleagues and some very friendly people who did everything to accommodate me and anyone who knows Australia will know just how generous in spirit and welcoming Australians are (except during Ashes test matches!). Nonetheless it was an extremely hard decision to make, but having made that decision I now appreciate just how small the world is. The knowledge that the United Kingdom is only 20 hours away made things a lot easier initially. Think about that! Twenty hours away: it is quicker to fly from Sydney to London than it is to get between one junction and the next on the M25 in the rush hour these days! Or, in fact, anywhere in the West Country on a bank holiday. So no matter where you are moving to, the world is a small place and with telecommunications and email and regular flights it really does not have to be an issue for you and you can always move back if change your mind.

Family and friends

You have to appreciate the support that you can enjoy from your family and friends and the support that you give your family and friends. But equally you have to recognize that basing your decision solely on that, on those people, is essentially saying that you are totally dependent on those people for your happiness. This is a dangerous position to be in, because there is nothing stopping those people moving elsewhere themselves! While you have foregone all the fantastic opportunities because you feel you don't want to break up the group or move away, you might then turn around and find that your friends are going to do exactly that to you! You will be particularly unhappy about that! In other words, you can't rely on those other people for all your personal happiness and if this is a good opportunity for you it is worth taking. It doesn't mean that you won't see these people again and it doesn't mean that you won't be able to keep in touch with those people. And of course, you can keep in touch and visit when you return home.

Doubts like worries are inevitable when you are deciding whether to stay or go. The danger is that you take the fact that you are having doubts as a potent sign that you shouldn't be moving. If you choose to interpret your doubts in that way, you are never even going to get out of bed in the morning, because you are always going to have doubts about how well the day is going to go and doubts about whether it will rain or not. So, doubts do not indicate anything other than the fact that you are human and like all humans you are bound to have doubts about your performance.

Of course, doubts after the fact are also a very common experience, that kind of sinking feeling and butterflies in the stomach feeling that people can get on having made the decision and having committed themselves to a course of action and then have second thoughts. A very common experience for people who go shopping is the adrenalin rush that is associated with purchasing something and then that feeling of I didn't want that, why did I go and do that? Do I really need this? This is followed by a period of justification and argument with yourself while you try to convince yourself that in fact whatever it is that you purchased was absolutely essential and you really couldn't have led your life without it. Now, of course, this is just an illusion as are many other sorts of doubt and trying to get into the idea that you absolutely had to have something or didn't have something isn't correct.

The fact that you are moving to a new job and thinking I am not sure if I should be doing this is perfectly normal. You are challenging the situation. The trouble is that people should be having those second thoughts in their current jobs, they should be thinking why am I still here? But they don't do it. They only tend to do that when they move to a new job and then say what have I got myself into? When you start thinking along these lines, the temptation to bolt is enormous. The temptation to give it all up or resign in the first month or two when something doesn't work out as planned can be very strong and can be a very tempting option for some people. Clearly, it is *not* a good move and one of the reasons why it is not a good move is that as a rule of thumb you should be looking to spend at least six months and, much more preferably, about 12 months in each job you go into. So when you move into a new job you have to think of it as a 12-month commitment at the least and you should be thinking, generally speaking, unless it is contract work in terms of a two- to three-year commitment in any one organization, with a review at 12 months, 18 months and certainly one at 3 years.

Worries and doubts are integral to nearly all decisions about whether to stay or go. By all means think through the worries and doubts, but act on them to modify them. This is the critical difference. Rather than just entertaining those worries and doubts get yourself into a problem-solving mode. Instead of saying, it could all go wrong, this could be terrible, say to yourself, how could it go wrong, what are the realistic things that could go wrong, what are the totally unrealistic things that could go wrong?

One of the totally unrealistic things that could go wrong is that you get killed by the boss's cat, as you swerve to miss him in the driveway at the boss's house when he invites you to a cocktail party and you end up with your car wrapped around his tree and you die. That's clearly high unlikely to happen and therefore you can dismiss that one out of hand (er, I think . . .).

So entertain worries and doubts by all means, but use them to plan possible solutions to problems and you will find yourself getting much more competent in whatever decision you choose to take.

PART FOUR

Staying put

In this part of the book, I look at how to ensure your decision to stay, once made, pays off for you.

CHAPTER ELEVEN

Making your stay successful

So you have decided to stay put! If you are going to stay you need to make some decisions and some agreements with yourself about how you are going to perform. If you are going to stay in the job, you may as well try to be as successful as you possibly can be. Otherwise, why stay? If work is important to you then you should be trying the best you possibly can for yourself. Not necessarily for your employer, but for your own self-esteem and for your reputation because there may be a time in the future when you do want to move and therefore it is important that you keep working at a high-quality level to maximize your chances of moving in the future. Equally a job well done is intrinsically satisfying. So how do you make your staying in one place successful?

Keep it under your hat

First, you can make your stay successful by not advertising to all and sundry that you were thinking of leaving in the first place (quick, the boss is coming, put this book under the table . . . if having Jim Bright on your lap is not a totally revolting suggestion!). If you are genuinely thinking of leaving then you really should not advertise the fact. There is a layman's view about suicide that those people who threaten it on a regular basis are the least likely to do it merely because the true intention is not to commit suicide but to get some attention. However, you also see this kind of behaviour in the workplace, where people are constantly making threats to leave and it essentially amounts to nothing more than empty rhetoric. After about the fourth or fifth occasion of making this threat the person can be treated with some degree of disdain and reasonably safely can be ignored. A colleague may come up and say: 'You know when you said you were about to leave if such and such didn't happen, well it didn't happen and you are still here!' You can look very silly when people say that sort of thing and it is your fault for sounding off with empty threats. So, if you *are* going to stay get out of the habit of making threats about leaving, don't draw lines in the sand and limit your behaviour by saying if this doesn't happen, if I don't get my demands, then I am going to leave.

Discretion in deciding whether to stay or go is so very important. If you do decide to stay you don't want that to be interpreted by either your friends or, more important, by potential competitors or employees as showing a sign of weakness on your part. You don't want to get into a situation where people begin to think that you will never leave because that can fatally undermine your credibility within the organization. I can think of a colleague who (unbeknown to her) has been labelled as unlikely ever to leave. As a result of that I have noticed that she has been treated extremely badly by the management in her organization. They think (perhaps rightly) that they have her over a barrel and this is the best possible job for her at the moment and there is no chance of her leaving; neither would she necessarily get a job elsewhere. Consequently, they can use that information to deny her promotion and pay rises. So, you don't want to advertise the fact that you are looking and then decide not to go somewhere, because such information could be used against you. The other side of this equation is the other employers who might think: 'Oh well, she came along, she played footsy with us but ultimately she didn't go through and commit. We wasted at lot of time and resources doing that, but the person simply didn't want to move!' A very public failure to take an opportunity can lead to people getting labelled. They can be seen as fussy, timewasters, indecisive, wedded to the familiar or enjoying a sinecure.

Do not live in the past

You need to state the view that the past is the past. There is no point in getting into the 'what might have been' state. There is nothing more boring than listening to somebody recounting for the umpteenth time: 'I could have been better off! I could have accepted that invitation from Stephen Spielberg, I would have been famous now and living on that 10 million dollar yacht and I would have had that house in Malibu.' This is all very well, but they are overlooking the key fact that they didn't take that decision. If anything, such statements just broadcasts their stupidity!

The past is the past and the offers are no longer on the table; you have declined them, you decided to stay put and stop looking. It would be good to think that you have thought through all the processes we have talked about so far and this is the right decision for you. You now need to get into a period of further consolidating or developing your career. You should still be looking from time to time for other jobs, but this does not mean necessarily looking over your shoulder at the organizations you were looking at before. If you have assessed those companies appropriately and they were not right for you at the time then it is time to move on to other companies and considerations when next the occasion rises.

Who cares who took the job – you certainly shouldn't

Don't look enviously at the individual who took up whatever offer that you declined. You don't want to end up like the Decca record company that turned down the Beatles for a recording contract. Not the most clued-up piece of management decision making!

You can use your new resolution to stay in the company, a bit like the person renewing their marriage vows and entering into the next stage of their life with renewed vigour, determination and motivation. If you have made a clear commitment to stay with the organization you want to build on that commitment. Use it to recharge your batteries and feel confident and happy that you are in fact in the best available job at the time. You can see where this is going? If you are having doubts of whether you are in the best job possible, it probably means you haven't done your thinking properly in the first place about the decision and you may have made the wrong decision! If you are feeling like that then you need to go back and go through the process a bit more rigorously of considering the other possibilities set out earlier.

Bear in mind that if you *are* going to stay, you mustn't fall into the trap of absolutist thinking: it doesn't mean that you have to stay there forever more. It doesn't have to mean that you are going to spend the rest of your working life there. Clearly, if you are getting close to retirement then the chances are that you will see out this part of your life with the company. But there is no reason not to think of this laterally and there is no reason why you couldn't go into business on your own or run a shop or do 101 other things once you get to the formal retirement age. Again, it is a way of thinking about your decisions and getting away from the absolutist self-limiting talk.

Don't forget to review yourself

Once you have made a decision to stay you should put in place some review points to consider whether to move or not! That may sound a little contrary, but the point is that you must always actively manage your career and that means taking stock from time to time. If you have just been through significant soul searching about staying or going, then by all means put off any more serious consideration of moving, perhaps for a period of about six to eight months. Obviously, you should not completely ignore any possible options or opportunities that arise, but you may not necessarily want to go actively looking for them. If you have been through a particularly painful, soul-searching and highly disruptive period then a period of stability is probably going to help your work performance which in turn is going to help your career prospects and career options in the longer term. It will also take the pressure off.

However, what you should be doing is putting in place some personal goals and achievements:

- What do you expect to achieve over the next 12 months to make your job more satisfying?
- What can you do to increase your skills?
- What can you do to increase your longer term employability during this period?
- Does the job live up to the expectations you had when you decided to stay?

Stick to your guns (for a while at least!)

Set yourself some goals if you are planning to stay and stick to those goals. Generally speaking, you should stay in any position for at least 12 months before you move on, otherwise you are going to have difficulty explaining the regular turnover on your résumé. There are exceptions to this, of course, periods under three months can generally be hidden easily enough; if the company is heading for disaster and some mud might stick if you stay; if you live in an area with poor job prospects and you have reliable information that large-scale layoffs are coming you might want to abandon ship to be at the front of the job queue before your colleagues (and given you've not been there that long you won't be sacrificing much in the way of redundancy payments).

However, if you have been with the company for a period of time already and you have just decided against moving on, don't then immediately review your decision. That applies especially in times of stress where it is tempting to blame work for your feelings. Don't think about making a decision for at least three to four months. This is not dissimilar to the advice given to dieters that they should refrain from continually weighing themselves. To do so risks the possibility that you will lose motivation due to minor upward fluctuations in weight. In the same way, if every irritant or perceived slight at work leads to a full-scale assessment of your prospects you risk becoming consumed by this decision and it will distract you from your daily tasks. In the same way that the dieter gets a more accurate indication of where their weight is going by weighing themselves periodically, you will have a better idea where your future lies if you review where you are at (say) quarterly intervals.

So, if you are going to commit to staying then put your nose down, work hard, set yourself some goals, work hard towards those goals and don't ruminate over what might have been.

Regular CAR maintenance (check, action, review)

Treat your career like a new motor car. After three months your car has a light service, the oil is changed and everything is given a quick once over to check that you have the requisite number of wheels etc.! Then, every year or two, you give your pride and joy a more thorough overhaul to check all is working properly. This schedule is not a bad model for your career.

Check (quarterly)

Every quarter, conduct just a brief check. Make time to ask yourself the following questions:

- Are you coping with your work?
- Are you maintaining your work standards?
- Do you expect your work to stay the same over the next three months?
- How is your home-work balance?
- Are you on track towards your goals?
- What refinements to your goals should you make?
- What additional goals should you include?
- What sorts of jobs are on offer in the market?
- How can you improve your life over the next three months?
- What ideas or feelings should you take note of to review at the end of the year?

Action (yearly – biannually)

- Meet key contacts to discuss opportunities, the labour market in general.
- Ascertain what your competitors and potential employers are doing – new projects, directions and approaches.
- Attend a major professional development activity such as a training workshop or conference.

- Volunteer for a work or non-work activity (such as a community pro-gramme) where you can develop a new skill or maintain an existing skill you don't get to use in your current role (e.g. public speaking, coaching and mentoring, sales and marketing, managing a team, helping people, customer service etc.).

- Spend significant time (e.g. a day or more) searching key job websites and company websites for information about jobs and industries.

Review (yearly – biannually)

You should complete the check inventory (p. 106) and also the personal and organizational audits described in chapter 5. You should also go over your quarterly checks and reflect on any ideas or feelings that have arisen in that process.

CHAPTER TWELVE

Getting promoted

If you are going to stay put then you may as well make every possible effort to maximize your opportunities within the organization rather than going elsewhere. There are three essential methods of getting on in a career. One is to make regular moves, the second way is to stay within the organization and third is to star in *Neighbours*. Conventional wisdom has it, and research backs up the proposition, that you can move higher up the ladder by moving from one company to another than you can on the internal ladder. Contrary to the popular view that suggests that the jobs are only for the boys and inside candidates have a stronger chance, research indicates that people who come into an organization at a higher level move up it faster. So those that start at the bottom expecting to move up have got a long and possibly gruelling path ahead of them, perhaps blocked on regular occasions by the new boys and girls on the block.

However, many people do stay with a particular organization because it might offer a whole range of tangible and intangible benefits associated with staying that would not be necessarily available elsewhere such as an excellent superannuation scheme, a childcare scheme, particular holidays or bonus cars, a whole range of different things, possibility of long-service leave and so on, that makes staying worthwhile (see Chapter 7 for a more complete list). If you *are* going to stay then you should be seriously thinking of promotion.

Getting promoted within an organization varies from organization to organization and from industry sector to industry sector. It also varies across private and public sector organizations. Public sector organizations tend to have long, arduous and extensive promotions procedures which very often include panel interviews and submissions of lots of documentation. The upside to this process is that the promotion process is relatively transparent in comparison to some private sector practices and in theory should be more about meeting objective performance standards and less about personalities (naïve twit that I am!). However, get a performance system, put it in the hands of a human being and I shall show you a totally corrupted and distorted system. We all have our likes and dislikes and therefore if you are going to be promoted it is a very good idea to understand the rules of the game and to understand where the threats are likely to come from and how it can work for you.

Get a friend or Godfather

One of the most powerful and sensible things to do if you are looking for promotion is to find yourself an influential mentor and supporter within the organization. Finding a senior individual within the company who will speak up on your behalf on occasions or who could even be on your interview panel is going to assist you greatly. Such figures can help by putting your name in the hat when options come up, speaking highly of you and generally being aware of your work and achievements. Here are some tips about doing this:

- Identify people in your organization who you feel may be able to provide you with a leg up (NB: not necessarily 'over').
- Make yourself useful to your sponsor.
- Work with or for your sponsor when you can.
- Get to meet your sponsor at company dos and social occasions.
- Try to get your sponsor aware of the sorts of work you are doing.
- Send your sponsor copies of projects you are working on or your sales figures.
- Ask your sponsor for their opinion and advice directly with issues that you might be facing at work.

Many sponsors in these circumstances will be flattered that you are asking these questions, if it is done in a positive, developmentally focused manner as opposed to a whining way. So instead of saying 'Oh God, I can't sell this product, it's rubbish and no one wants to buy it' try saying 'I created a whole range of techniques to improve my sales and I have met with some mixed success there, I know you used to work in this job some years before. What would you say are the most important attributes for people doing well in this job and what was your secret to success?'

People love to be asked questions like that because it indicates a level of respect and acknowledgement and understanding of their career achievements and people are much more likely to be generous with their time in providing this kind of information. The very fact that you are listening to a more senior person is a positive sign and it is likely to lead to them forming a very favourable impression. This is all to your good in terms of getting promoted!

Know the rules of the game you are playing

I mentioned in the chapter about making your stay successful that you should be looking at setting goals in relation to your work achievements and looking to do the best possible job you can. For most situations, talent will win out and having a series of achievements that you can point to at work is the most surefire way of gaining a promotion. Consequently, keeping a series of achievements is important. Second it is important to understand the rules of the game in terms of promotion. You need to understand in your environment what the basis for promotion is. In public service jobs, military jobs, academic jobs and some large organizations, the basis of promotion is usually explicitly set out in a series of job descriptions and the process of promotion is also set out by human resources. Avail yourself of that information at the earliest opportunity so you know exactly what is required in terms of getting promoted. Try to identify colleagues who have gone through the process successfully in the recent past and try to gain from them some ideas and some tips as to how you might go about doing it. Understand the rules of promotion and understand the criteria of promotion. Truly try and understand the criteria and ask and get clarification from supervisors and people who have been through that process as soon as possible on any point that you may not be sure about. Even for the points on which you feel sure, go back and check, question and challenge your thinking to see whether there may be other interpretations. It can be very easy to look at the criteria and convince ourselves that we more than exceed these only to be disappointed when a different interpretation is put on them or we are subject to a line of particularly aggressive questioning that reveals that, in fact, we don't genuinely meet some of the criteria.

Orient your behaviour toward known performance standards

Understand what the performance criteria are and use them to set the tone and direction of your behaviour. If this is what the company rewards then that it is the sort of behaviour that you should give them. It is no point going out on a limb and doing something that you think is tremendously important if, according to the promotional guidelines, that stuff is of no consequence or merit in the organization and it doesn't count very strongly or at all towards your promotion. By all means do things which don't go towards your promotion but do recognize that by putting energy into those things you are potentially reducing your chances and opportunity of pro-motion because that energy could be more productively put into promo-tion-related criteria. So know the rules and also know the process and get some idea of the likelihood of promotion. Ask these questions:

- How often have people in your position been promoted in the past?
- Is promotion something that is relatively routine?
- How long have people in the past served in your level and position before they get promoted?
- How often have people had to apply for promotion before they finally get it? (Good to know when handling rejection.)

Rejection and motivation

It is tempting to start thinking that your company doesn't value you because you have not been promoted. It can be extremely demotivating for anyone when this happens. You have to remind yourself that this is a game and it is often in the employers' interests not to promote because they want you to work for the least amount of money that they can get away with paying you. A promotion is almost inevitably associated with pay increases. No employer of any guile is voluntarily going to increase staff wages if they don't have to. It makes absolutely no sense, especially if they are account-able to a board or shareholders.

Consequently, don't expect your boss, supervisor or mentor to invite you to go for promotion. Equally, it is a totally unrealistic expectation to sit there like a wallflower waiting to be asked to go for promotion. No company is sensibly going to do that; rather, you have to take the initiative and apply for it. Now of course this means you have to set yourself up for a situation in which you may possibly fail. One of the themes of this book is that the constant avoidance of situations where you might fail, the fear of failure, is one of the most potent self-limiting factors which can severely restrict people's careers.

It may well be the culture in your organization that you have to apply several times before you ultimately get promoted to the position you want. Sometimes this is a bit of kidology by the company which really wants to ensure that you are genuinely grateful when you finally get it and therefore suitably motivated. It may be that they want to try and maintain a level of superiority and seniority around particular positions and therefore they don't want to make them seem too attainable. Whatever the motivations, do not forget the game playing that surrounds these decisions from time to time.

It's time

It could be that the first time you apply you simply are not quite ready. You haven't quite got in place the full portfolio of skills, achievements and experience that is required for the role. It is often not a bad idea to have a 'trial run' at promotion, providing you can avoid beating yourself up with self-limiting thoughts if it is unsuccessful. This way you will go through the process and get experience. If you approach it with the expectation that you will be extremely lucky to get it, failing is no disgrace, you can learn a lot from the experience of putting together your promotion application, rehearsing the argument of the basis of your promotion. The experience of going through the promotion interview to get some insight into the sort of things that your organization values and the lines of questioning and style of the interviews will serve you in good stead next time around. So it's not a bad idea to apply for promotion in a speculative way, providing the speculation is not totally unrealistic.

Given that promotion is not all that easy to get, applying for it can be seen as a very positive sign by management and it is an indication of your ambition. It may also show to them your potential and the fact that you are seeing yourself working at the next level. Therefore this may put into their minds the possibility that you may also be looking to find jobs at that level elsewhere and this can also help you. Putting your achievements under the noses of management is not a bad thing to do on a regular basis, because it means that they will be aware of you and they will be aware of the quality of your work which may not be apparent if you just sit back and wait until the promotion is offered to you.

PART FIVE

Making the move

In this part I cover the sorts of preparation and consideration required to make the transition to your new job. Moving jobs can be as stressful as moving house and, like moving house, it is easy for things to suffer lasting damage if the move is not organized properly.

CHAPTER THIRTEEN

Preparing for the big day

So, you have decided to make the move – congratulations! You are going to embark on a new and exciting phase in your life. How do you now plan for the big day? What should you be doing in order to make the move a success?

Timing and dates

First, you have to decide about the timing of your resignation. You may have negotiated a start date with the company you are going to or you know the date of the course you are going to enrol in or when you have got to get on your yacht to sail around the world or whatever else you may be doing other than working in your old job! Bearing that in mind you need to work out the optimum date for you to leave your job and there are several factors that come into this. If you are working in a safety critical or security critical kind of job such as computing work which involves managing finances or similar then do not be surprised if you are asked to leave the building the moment you announce your resignation. This is because companies are anxious that you may get involved in corrupting the software or copying confidential information if you hang around once you have made a commitment to another organization or even a competitor. So, in these circumstances, you really have to decide whether or not you are ready to go immediately, *before* making the announcement.

It is important to check your contract that may stipulate a period of notice that is required to be given. Ideally, you would have done this before you have finally made your decision or before you have committed to another employer or another course of action. This can be a contentious issue. For some jobs, the period of notice can be relatively long. It can be up to six months in teaching and academic jobs, for instance. The degree to which you work your notice and give your notice depends on the degree to which the contract is enforced. It varies considerably across companies, some insisting you work every last second and others happy for you to push off pretty much immediately despite what it says in the contract. Why have an uncommitted employee hanging around possibly undermining morale, when they could start the rehire process without delay? Typically, one month's notice is required in most organizations. However, if push comes to shove many organizations will not attempt to enforce that period of time and, generally speaking, you can more or less walk out when you please. The worse that can possibly happen is that you may find that you lose some benefits or salary. If you think you are going to leave fairly rapidly you might want to consider trying to get the timing right to ensure that you have just been paid so that your pay is relatively up to date (see money considerations earlier in the book). For people who are working in arrears this can be problematic. But again by getting your timing right you can minimize the amount of your pay that the company may hold in lieu of your working your notice.

Also bear in mind that you may have possibly accrued holiday leave or long-service leave and this can be taken into account as well in terms of the final day of service. You may wish to have your holiday leave paid out but equally you may want to take your leave. For instance, if you have got seven days of holiday owing to you and you have got a month's notice, then you could quite reasonably work two-and-a-half more weeks and take a week and bit of holiday at the end of that. Ultimately, it's very rarely in the employers' interest to hold you in the company and hold you to work against your will. If relationships between you and the company have broken down to that extent, then most cluey managers will simply let you go rather than have the pain of an extremely reluctant employee there who may, in fact, be more trouble than they are worth. However, do consider what I have to say in the next chapter about burning bridges and hopefully you will avoid getting into that situation.

Other factors that you may want to take into consideration in terms of timing is how your role may change during the transition or resignation period. I have known of colleagues in consulting firms who, on announcing their resignation, have been humiliated by having been moved out of their office that same day and put into a corridor with a desk by the lift while the senior partner personally took a screwdriver to their office door nameplate to expunge any trace of said employee! One colleague of mine did not envisage this childish and petulant behaviour (although why he should have had a high opinion of this partner I have never understood!) and he was most hurt at this brutal kind of treatment.

By resigning you are creating problems for the organization and you are possibly, in a most public way, rejecting them. In most cases the organization will need to find a replacement. That will take them time and cost them money and it will distract them from their normal work. Further, they have got to find some way of covering the work that you won't be doing. So, it's a disruptive process and don't expect people necessarily to respond positively or think about your interests at such times.

If you are working on a particular project or you have some colleagues either within the organization or within the industry and you have made some promises or commitments to those people do seriously consider fulfilling those as best you possibly can. Also appreciate that one possibility of resigning is that you may be removed from a whole heap of projects and be unable to fulfil your different commitments and therefore you may end up letting people down.

Equally, do not expect your employer to honour things like travel and attendance at conferences. It is not at all unheard of for companies to refuse to honour commitments to send resigning staff to conferences, training courses or overseas trips. Again this can be sometimes the petty managers who want to get their own back for you resigning, but equally the company may take the view that there is nothing to be gained by their paying for you to do these things; it is not in their interests for you to do it and therefore they don't want it.

Generally speaking, the more notice you can give to people and the more consideration and assistance you can give to people, the better and smoother it is all round. If you have been working for an organization for a long time, however temping it may be to start a complaint it is much better to leave on a positive note and leave people wanting more than leaving on a sour note (see next chapter).

So, putting in place sound planning for the day is a sensible activity. If you want to be appreciated on leaving, you can start quietly and discretely (assuming you have not yet announced your move) to put in place procedure manuals and clear documentation of where and what things exist. This will help people who might do your job in transit or in fact help the new incumbent in that position.

People often feel they have ownership over their role and therefore they feel (especially managers) they have a role as kingmaker – to nominate or choose their successor. Don't be at all surprised if management don't appear to take on board your recommendations as to who should take on your role. Given the political nature of work it is inevitable that people who you disagree with or people who want to get their own back for your resignation may well decide that they don't want anything to do with 'your sorts' of people or they may want to make use of the opportunity to put in place one of their own men rather than somebody from your team. Consequently, if you have people who are working with you, you may want to point out to them that it may not be necessarily the best thing they ever do to identify themselves too closely with you as it may jeopardize their chances of getting your position when you do go. If you seriously think that your view will not only be discounted but will also provoke people to take the opposite course of action, then you could always make some deliberately contrary recommendations. But it is much better all round to leave the decision making to those who have an ongoing commitment to the organization. It is no longer your role.

The other sort of planning that you ought to put in place is that, generally speaking, any sort of moves, like moving house, moving units, moving kids from school to school or moving jobs involves expense. Therefore it is a good idea to get your financial house in order before you move. For instance, in moving jobs you may decide to try for a bit of an image makeover and some new clothes. They may be unique new clothes given the demands of the new work. It may be some form of uniform or a different coloured wardrobe required; it may be you have to wear a suit where before you wore casual clothes. Alternatively, it could be that you need some more casual clothes where before you were wearing a suit. It could be a whole range of things like that and very often people just want to start off in their new job with some new clothes. If that is your view, then it will cost money and the cost of a business suit these days is not inconsiderable and you may well want to account for that.

Second, when you do move to a new job you can anticipate there may be social functions that you get invited to or induction events and again these will probably involve some costs and you do want to have at the very least some money to be able to pay your share if you go out for a meal. It may be also that you need to get to meet new clients and customers and although this may be something that the organization should pay for, they may not, and if you want to improve your effectiveness quickly you may find yourself popping out regularly for coffees or sandwiches, lunch or dinner with potential clients who can assist you in your job and this means some form of personal investment of your own funds in doing that. Equally, it may be that you have different transport costs or demands placed on you in your new role which might necessitate your buying a car or a more reliable car. It may mean you have to buy yourself a season ticket or a more expensive season ticket. So there could be changes there which need more expenditure and again getting your finances in order before you go is a good move.

If there is a small gap in ceasing your employment in one place and starting in another you will need some way of making sure you can cover that space when you are not being paid. Other problems can come in, in terms of frequency of pay. If you have been paid on a weekly or fortnightly basis moving to a company that pays on a monthly basis can create cash flow problems which can take a long time to overcome. Getting some freedom on your credit card, either by increasing the limit or preferably paying off the card in total or in part to cover essentials during the transition period is also an extremely good idea.

At work you should go through your files carefully and if you have a computer you should go through your computer files very carefully and start removing any personal files which have found their way on there. This includes personal emails. You don't want people writing to your personal correspondents after you leave or reading any correspondence left on the computer. So, you should go through and remove all those emails. Second, once you have announced within the company of what you are doing you should have in place a strategy to inform all of your clients and customers that you are moving. It is unethical to steal a company's customers and clients and many contracts, particularly in consulting, often include clauses which say that you will not approach your old customers and clients for business. However, this does not preclude you from (and nobody can really stop you from) contacting customers and clients to inform them that you will no longer be working for the company. Furthermore, it is perfectly reasonable for you to provide contact details should they wish to contact you. The contract may preclude your contacting them, but there is nothing that can be done legally to prevent clients and customers choosing to contact you and providing a contact address is not doing anything other than providing a courtesy to those people. You may have some unfinished business with those people. Of course, if they do decide to come with you all the better, but that is their decision and not yours.

So, leaving a tidy desk and a clear desk is a good idea and equally it is a good idea to try to get projects completed. It may well be that you strive to finish projects before you publicly announce that you are going and again that can soften the blow for people because you can explain when you do resign that you have put in extra time or overtime to get these projects out of the way and therefore to make things easier on the company in the transition period and perhaps easier for the successor who doesn't have to pick up half-finished work. Also, you may try and put in place a fairly systematic filing procedure so your successor will not have a hard time in working out what needs to be done. All this sets up a very good impression in the organization and it all helps you leave on a high note with high regard.

Leaving functions

You may also consider whether or not you want a leaving do and some organizations will routinely offer this to you and others will not. Leaving presents is another problem in organizations. In organizations with high turnover continual whiprounds for presents can be a particular issue because employees may resent the steady flow of their cash to departing colleagues. So think through the possibility that (a) you may not be getting that fully equipped 34ft yacht as your leaving present after all and (b) bear in mind that leaving presents will tend to reflect the amount of time that you have been with the organization. Just assume that you are going to be given a completely disgusting tasteless painting done by the boss's dentist and something like a pot plant that will die before you get home.

The leaving do as well can be problematic and these things are always extremely embarrassing for the people involved. They will range from drinks on the desk in the office, to a meal at a hotel, right through to a full-scale party. If you leave at Christmas, expect a small ceremony during the Christmas party. However, don't get into the feeling of expectation no matter what traditions may have been in the past and how many you have been to. It is completely pointless to measure your self-worth in terms of how many people turn up or the cost of the event and so on. Equally, if you are going to go to something like that just be careful of behaving yourself. I have heard some of the most extraordinarily bad leaving speeches and equally the most extraordinarily and inadvertently insulting speeches given by people corralled to say something nice about the individual concerned. Leaving dos are often awkward events for all concerned. Don't put too much emphasis on having fun; it is something you should get through with your dignity intact and hopefully with your mouth shut if there is any temptation to say anything negative.

CHAPTER FOURTEEN

Burning bridges and maintaining ties

Don't burn the one and do maintain the other

The very fact that you have made a clear decision of whether you stay or go is often reason enough to feel elated and confident and generally pretty pleased with yourself. In addition to that your mood has probably improved because you have in your own mind extracted yourself from the situation that has become less than ideal. After all why are you leaving in the first place if everything was ideal at work? Now the decision is made you are moving into a new and potentially dangerous phase and, that is, justifying the decision. We have already discussed the often very irrational behaviour and emotions that go into making a decision of this sort and consequently trying to search for an underlining objective rational reason for making the decision is going to be pretty fruitless on many occasions. That is why we take so long to make the decision in the first place and why the decision can be so hard.

Sometimes, having made the decision we now feel that we have got the insight of a prophet and we are able to find countless reasons why we are leaving and, of course, all those reasons will focus on the shortcomings of your current position, your boss, colleagues and perhaps the products too! The temptation to slag off all your colleagues, slag off the company and slag off your boss can be irresistible.

People often think for some bizarre reason that slagging off the workplace is exactly what their colleagues want to hear. The trouble is if you think about that for a second, your colleagues have not decided to leave, your colleagues are staying there. Even if the workplace appears totally awful in many respects your colleagues may not be able to leave for whatever reason. They may have gone through exactly the same process that you have, they may not be as well qualified or they may not have the profile that you have which allows you to leave. They may have different personal or financial circumstances which makes it difficult for them to leave. They may have different opinions about the company's process and products. There is a whole host of reasons why those people either do not or cannot leave the organization. So your turning around and highlighting to them all the deficiencies in that organization and the people in it is inadvertently rubbing their noses in the situation.

Alternatively, they may not share your opinions and all you are doing in that case is highlighting your lack of insight or other personal shortcomings and not those of the organization. The following box contains a classic example of this kind of thinking:

> A friend of mine went for an interview to be a secretary and she was asked how many days had she had off in the previous year through sickness. Now that seems like a pretty straightforward question. She figured the best way to make her look good was to distance herself from her current employer, making out that she didn't really like him and she didn't really want to be there (implication in her mind: I want to work for you and not them). So she tells the interviewer that she had loads of days off and was hardly ever at work! She was surprised when she didn't get the position.

The justification of our decision to leave is a psychological method of detaching and distancing ourselves from the organization we worked for. This is a major issue after all we may have been there many years and given a lot of our lives and a lot of our time. There has to be a good reason for all that time and for its coming to an end, so we search for plausible explanations. The easiest way to do that is to lash out and convince yourself that the organization is absolutely appalling. It is easier than living with the ambiguity that the old job had many good points, some of which will be sacrificed in the new job.

From a purely tactical point of view it is never a good idea to criticize other people in public. The entertainer Jimmy Durante said: 'Be nice to people on the way up because you will meet them all on the way down' and that is the same as regards to your career, because if you slag off your boss publicly, how do you know that he will not turn up in your new company? Second, those criticisms can reflect back on yourself – if they say that about others what do they say about me? If your colleagues can identify closely with the workplace, attacks on it can be taken to be attacks on them. Third, nobody likes a bore. People move jobs regularly. For you it may be a major event but it is not a unique phenomenon. Across the workforce people are doing it all the time and although this is an important and interesting moment in your life, don't expect other people to show their interest for that reason alone.

Next, today's target of your venom could be your customers or your clients in future. People tend to move within the same industry or the same general broad area – especially white-collar professional levels. That means that you are likely to mix with the same colleagues over long periods of time. For instance, in the consulting world it is very common for a consultant to move from one company to another. There is a lot of movement in that situation and therefore getting into character assassinations each time you leave a firm will guarantee you are going to be bumping into a lot of people who are now new-found enemies and your reputation will be one of disloyalty and indiscretion. Both these characteristics are fatal in consultants. Being outspoken in that setting is a very dangerous thing to do because you never know who you are going to need as an alliance partner or as a client, customer or as an employer in the future.

Finally, such abuse can be seen as a sign of emotional immaturity. Really emphasizing the emotional elements of the workplace and personal rivalries or disagreements is likely to highlight to others the extent to which you make your decisions based on emotion as opposed to logic. Also, do not make the mistake of assuming people will automatically see things your way. How often have you heard a person in the midst of a dispute trying to rally you to their cause by making out that the other party is totally unreasonable and irrational? And what view did you take? Probably like everyone else the balanced relatively impartial view. You probably see the merit in what they are saying, but you probably also recognize the exaggeration and the distortion that people put in there in order to convince themselves of their righteousness.

Another trap is in attacking the products of your old company as it can be treated as a sign of disloyalty. If you do this to your new employer in the first few weeks on the job, while initially it can be fun to listen to hair-raising and scandalous tales, after a while your audience may tend to start questioning the motives of the individual saying this stuff. They may question what you might say about this job when you leave the company and should you therefore be trusted? I think it was Dorothy Parker who said: 'If you have got something bad to say about people come and sit next to me.' They all like to hear the gossip but after a while people become tired of it and question your motives.

Burning your bridges can also pose a problem in the short term as well. Many people like to work out their notice in an organization. If you decide to go in there in a smug manner, hell bent on causing disruption or arguments or refusing to take directions from supervisors, you are going to make your last few weeks in the organization particularly unpleasant for your colleagues and your supervisor and, ultimately, for yourself. You need to question why you want retribution so dearly:

● Is it helping you?
● Does it make you feel better and put you in a better position?
● How important are references to you?
● Do you need people to vouch for your behaviour and professionalism?

If this is the case, getting into that kind of behaviour really isn't a sensible idea. You may also be letting down your colleagues if the work that you do is of importance to the organization. It is extreme selfishness to underperform in those last weeks, because you could well be creating headaches for people you've worked with for perhaps many years and for people who provided you with support over the years.

It is far better to leave with dignity and with the belief that you have given your best to that company on each day that you were there. It also helps you in your new work as well if you maintain your work attitude and don't go on a mental holiday the minute you decide to quit. In doing that you are likely to find work difficult to get after a period of this kind of behaviour. Equally, during that period of slacking off you are likely to develop bad habits. You might cop some undesirable and negative feedback from your supervisors or from your colleagues which sticks in your mind and comes back to haunt you in a quiet moment of reflection. You will be surprised how those remarks come readily to mind and then serve to undermine you during moments of vulnerability. The way to expose yourself to that unnecessary criticism and feedback is by behaving badly in the first place. Don't do it!

References

References are a contentious issue in selection because employers really do not know how much store they can place by them. My experience in relation to references is that they are really used as a selecting out device, rather than a selecting in device. I have rarely heard of people getting recruited on the basis of impeccable references, far more likely people are selected out of the process on the basis of lukewarm, indifferent or plain bad references. Employers are getting a lot more sophisticated on how they collect references and how they use them for selection process. Generally, the days are long gone when you could personally approach and handpick your referees and get them to write statements which you attach to your application as a testimonial. Most organizations will not accept those anymore as they recognize the stuff you handpick will be laudatory.

Increasingly, organizations insist on speaking to somebody personally in relation to your performance. Many organizations now expect to be able to speak to your most recent manager and some of the reference checking can be quite extensive. I have been involved in 30-minute or more interviews by telephone about particular candidates. Many organizations now and certainly recruitment firms that work on their behalf will ask a series of structured questions designed to probe and explore your opinion of the individual. This is to get away from the halo affect of the statements along the lines of 'He's a good lad' or 'Great worker' and so on. This will include weaknesses. I have been asked on a number of occasions to volunteer the weakest points of several candidates. Given this is going to happen, employers recruited to do this interviewing can usually detect when a referee is providing false information or is exaggerating their descriptions of the candidate. Therefore if you do start behaving badly at work and your supervisor is subjected to this kind of scrutiny the original intention of providing you a half-decent reference quickly wears off and the recruiter is able from the non-committal responses to questions to determine that you are, in fact, not the ideal person. So dealing courteously and professionally with your colleagues and supervisor in the workplace is never to be underestimated because it can come back and bite you in so many different ways. To behave badly is really career suicide.

Don't count your chickens until they've crossed the road

The excitement and emotion of making the decision to leave is not the same thing as having another job and being interviewed for a job and having positive feedback about that interview is not the same thing as having the job. I can think of several instances which are quite tragic where people have applied for jobs, have been successful and performed very strongly in their interview – perhaps, too, in their psychological testing – and they have been offered a position. They have then indulged in some of the bridge-burning behaviours that I have already highlighted and have made themselves very unpopular at work only to find that the employing organization, which up to this point, has not made any firm legal commitment to this individual withdraws their offer. This can happen for several reasons. First, some organizations will tell candidates that the job is pretty much in the bag and all that is required is to get some references. I have known a lot of applicants who get knocked back at this stage. Consider an organization that might be taking on a lot of people. They may need five employees to start. It is possible that after they received all the applications they have six really strong candidates. Therefore your chances of getting the position are extremely high. Five out of six chances of getting the position. Only one person is going to miss out, but under those circumstances all it needs is one slightly hesitant voice, one slightly less than confident description of your work for you to be knocked out of the race. If the other five have got impeccable references it could be enough to knock you out of the race. So you can go from the position of being extremely confident with every reason that you had one of the best opportunities ever to be given the position and you may even have been told this much and then the whole thing comes crashing down – boom! What do you do now when you have burnt your bridges?

This can also happen if the company concerned goes bankrupt. I can think of an example where a financier in a major broking house was headhunted for a position. Having gone through an interview and testing process impressively, with every expectation of getting the position, was told at the last minute that the senior management based in New York had announced a potential merger resulting in the company's stocks being suspended and all recruitment activities being indefinitely suspended while they went through a process of due diligence. Now, the local managers were completely unaware of this, it was all conducted in great secrecy for obvious reasons. But where does that leave the candidate concerned? They were pretty much all but offered the position by the local manager and in good faith, but events overtook them and the position didn't become available.

In another tragic circumstance I can think of an individual who went for a job and was unsuccessful in getting it. He proceeded to slag off the new company which rejected him saying how awful they were and how unfair and how he wouldn't want to work for them anyway, only to find that the person they selected died before they could take that position and, guess what!, the person was second on the list and, of course, surprise surprise!, they ended up taking the job. This was damaging for their credibility and it was clearly a way of trying to save face publicly. So burning your bridges is generally a really bad idea. It's a bad idea for you personally and for your reputation also. Even if you think that none of this stuff will come back to haunt you, you'd be surprised how these things can catch up with you.

I can speak with personal experience on deciding to work on the other side of the world and although at times I felt that was a very big move, I soon discovered that in fact the world is a very small place and several things have occurred. For instance, I worked with a colleague who shared an office with a previously very close colleague of mine. I have supervised an individual who worked very closely with another colleague of mine. A whole variety of different people under different circumstances have popped up unannounced all of whom have worked with me at previous times in my life. So, don't think that even moving away from your home is going to reduce the chances that you may someday bump into somebody who knows about you. Finally, don't burn your bridges if you are not absolutely definite that you have a contract of employment. Burning your bridges is *not* a good exercise.

PART SIX

Different situations

In this final part of the book, I provide some tips to deal with some career catastrophes. Even if it doesn't apply to you, it may set your mind at rest if you worry that one day it might. I also offer (somewhat tongue in cheek) a few famous examples of getting the decision wrong!

CHAPTER FIFTEEN

What happens if ...

I get made redundant

One man's tragedy is another man's opportunity. That seems to be the thinking about redundancy these days. This reflects the fact that redundancy has been increasingly seen as a boon for some people in the workplace. There is a small, but growing segment of the workforce who have done really well out of redundancy. They have picked up a lump-sum cheque and promptly walked into (very often) better positions with another employer.

If you have been made redundant, you face a set of challenges. Sometimes, redundancy programmes are voluntary but frequently it is imposed. Therefore, you have good reason to feel cynical about the entire subject of employment and especially feel hostile to the employer who made you redundant.

If the redundancy is voluntary, you should treat it in the same way you would treat any stay–go decision and weigh up all the issues raised earlier in this book.

If the redundancy is involuntary, it is easy to lose confidence in your abilities and skills and suffer lowered self-esteem. The challenge here is to overcome that loss of self-esteem and look beyond the immediate situation. You must maintain your self-belief and appreciate that you have a lot to offer.

Although to some extent the decision has been made for you (assuming it was involuntary), the post-redundancy period can also be a good time for you to sit down and take stock of your current career path or whether there may be different avenues open to you. The redundancy payment might provide you an opportunity to start your own business. You could consider part-time work or job sharing if your finances allow it. Redundancy can have a bright side, particularly if it offers new career opportunities and opens doors to a new business venture.

I get sacked

If this happens, it is a done deal. You should seek legal or union advice immediately. However tempting, do not get into slanging matches and do not do anything that might undermine any potential case you might bring. Remember, even if the experience causes you to not want to work there again, that should not prevent you accessing any compensation that is due to you. Take a breath, get advice and then move on positively.

I storm out

The whole of this book has been devoted to trying to keep you out of these situations. In future work hard on recognizing the danger signs – the times when you feel that you are becoming angry or upset and work on strategies to control that situation. Time out, deep breathing exercises, sleeping on it, biting your lip, letting the other side win the battle (but not the war), thinking through the impact you will have on your loved ones, seeing things from their point of view – there are many ways to deal with such stress and many good books and experts that can assist you. Decisions made in a blue fit are not necessarily the best ones.

I have second thoughts

You need to identify whether the second thoughts are the inevitable anxiety responses to change and uncertainty or a profound sense of doing the wrong thing. If they are worrisome thoughts, then interpret these as being totally normal, totally expected and in no way are they a sign that something is wrong. If your thoughts fall into this category, you should actively challenge and think through your concerns. Have a look back to the chapter on worries and anxieties for some tips on how to do this.

If you are totally convinced you have made a terrible mistake there are two courses of action open to you. The first is to accept it, appreciate you have stuffed up and simply get on with your life. There is no point dwelling on it any longer if there is no possibility of retracting the error. If you think you are the first person to stuff up you are very mistaken. If you think others do not stuff up, you are equally mistaken. The worst thing to do now is to compound your error (hey, it means you are a human being!) and wallow in it. That is an even worse mistake!

If you feel there is hope (and why not? – there is always hope) then take steps to retrieve the situation. This may well involve asking for your old job back. If you have heeded the advice about your departure given earlier, the chances are increased that you will have left on good terms. If so, you must be in a better position to retrieve it. Immediately contact the relevant person, preferably a sponsor in your old organization and point out your mistake. If you can explain why it happened or why your thinking was awry that will help them understand the situation. If there are some extenuating circumstances then do not hesitate to set them out in full. For instance, I recently had a client who, under the mistaken medical diagnosis that he was dying, promptly left his job. He then overcame his condition and it turned out he could have stayed in his old role all along. Follow up a letter with a personal call and try and get to meet with your old supervisor or sponsor. Bear in mind that contacting the HR department may not be your best bet, especially if the firm is large as they may not know you and may therefore deal with you like any other applicant.

If you approach the company shortly after your departure, it may be that they have not appointed anyone else anyway. If they have, that person might be on a probation period and you never know your luck, once made aware of your renewed availability your supervisor might find previously unnoticed deficiencies in the new person's performance!

CHAPTER SIXTEEN

Some people who should either have stayed or gone – but didn't

Name	Mistake	Reason
Winston Churchill	Stayed – should have gone	Could never match his wartime success in a peacetime government
Geoff Boycott (cricketer)	Went – should have stayed home	Toured Australia in 1978–79 when not in the best frame of mind and played below his best – had he not gone his test batting average would have remained over 50!
Bob Hawke (Australian Prime Minister)	Stayed – should have gone	Promised to make way for Paul Keating but hung in and had power wrestled from him
Big Joe Duskin's father	Stayed too long!	Made his musician son promise not to play rhythm and blues while he lived. He then lived to be 104! His son kept his promise and worked in the post office instead!
The Rolling Stones	Stayed	Zimmerframe rock is not a good look
Stan Laurel (English comedian)	Did both and was wrong each time	Married seven times, three times to the same woman
Laurel and Hardy (English and US comedy duo)	Went – should have stayed	Left the studio where they had all their hits and ended up playing second fiddle to Abott and Costello
Morecombe and Wise (English comedians)	Went from the BBC to ITV	Were never the same force on commercial TV
Peter Sellars (English comedian and film actor)	Stayed	One *Pink Panther* film too many

Elizabeth Taylor and Richard Burton	Went, returned and went again	Couldn't make their minds up!
Frank Sinatra	Stayed	Threatened to cloud a great career with recordings after his voice had lost its magic
Just about any soap opera actor you care to mention	Stayed too long	Got typecast and when the axe fell could not find work
Kenneth Williams (English actor)	Stayed too long in *Carry On* films	What was he thinking of making *Carry On Emmanuel*?
Colin Huxley (my mate and vet)	Went and should have stayed	Left the Sydney Cricket Ground early to miss the rush and missed Darren Gough getting a hat trick

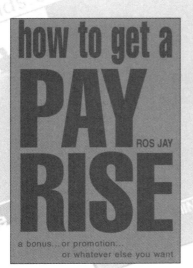

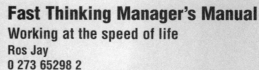

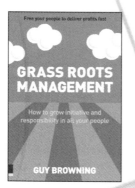

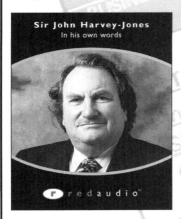